I N N E R
HARVEST

I N N E R
HARVEST

Hazelden
Publishing

First published February 1990.

Copyright © 1990, Hazelden Foundation.
ISBN-13: 978-0-89486-611-1
ISBN-10: 0-89486-611-7
Library of Congress Catalog Card Number:
89-84786
Printed in the United States of America.

About Hazelden Publishing

As part of the Hazelden Betty Ford Foundation, Hazelden Publishing offers both cutting-edge educational resources and inspirational books. Our print and digital works help guide individuals in treatment and recovery, and their loved ones. Professionals who work to prevent and treat addiction also turn to Hazelden Publishing for evidence-based curricula, digital content solutions, and videos for use in schools, treatment programs, correctional programs, and electronic health records systems. We also offer training for implementation of our curricula.

Through published and digital works, Hazelden Publishing extends the reach of healing and hope to individuals, families, and communities affected by addiction and related issues.

For more information about Hazelden publications,
please call 800-328-9000 or visit us online at
hazelden.org/bookstore.

January

A new year. A new day. A new beginning. How do we become new?

This year holds out the possibility that we can learn from the past but not be bound by it. That we can move away from self-defeating habits. That we can come to better understand how much is enough, especially how much food is enough. Not too much, not too little, just . . . enough.

As we learn how much food is enough, we can also learn how much is enough in other areas of life. How much work, how much play, how much money, how much sex, how many possessions.

We don't need to make resolutions for learning all of this perfectly. Resolutions can set us up for disappointment. We will not be perfect today or any day. But we can be open to the possibilities that this moment, this hour, and this day bring. Today we can look for new ways to respond to old problems. We can listen to our inner voice.

May today's new beginning be the next step in my recovery.

Hurts, fears, and food. Are they
related?

For many of us, emotional pain has been a signal to eat too much or too little. Unsure of how to express our feelings, we have numbed the pain by overeating or self-starvation. Neither route helps us deal with the pain.

Food is not very effective as a painkiller or anxiety reliever. When we eat for emotional reasons, we may feel better temporarily, but in the long run we do not solve our problems by overeating, nor can we starve them away.

If something hurts me today or if I'm afraid, I can give myself permission to feel my feelings, whatever they may be. I can talk to a friend, a family member, a counselor, or a support group. I can take one small step in the direction of experiencing my emotions more fully.

I will accept a hurt or fear today, feel it, and learn from it.

One is a whole number.

Feelings of inadequacy prompt us to do strange things. They prompt us to eat more than we need in an effort to fill an emotional void. They prompt us to lose more and more pounds in search of the "perfect" thinness, which eventually can become starvation. Feelings of inadequacy prompt us to compromise our needs and give up our integrity in an effort to please other people.

Somewhere along the line, many of us got the idea that we were not good enough just the way we were, by ourselves as individuals. We started thinking it was necessary to deny our feelings in order to have the approval of other people. As the food fog lifts, we see more clearly the roots of our feelings of inadequacy. Even more important, we are able to discard these old feelings and learn to value ourselves just as we are.

Through the Steps, we develop greater integrity. We become less dependent on external approval — validation from other people — and more confident of our own worth. With recovery, we become whole.

Today, I will be aware of my inner strength and integrity.

Choices — how do we make them?

Once we choose recovery, a vast new world of other choices begins to unfold. When we were caught in compulsion, we had relatively few choices available to us. With recovery from the food obsession comes more time and energy to devote to work relationships, hobbies, and just plain fun.

Increasingly, we have a new sense of freedom, which may well include some anxiety. How do we decide what to do today? How do we decide what to do with the time we formerly spent binge-ing, starving, and being obsessive about food? With whom do we want to spend it? In recovery, we have a wider range of choices to make about activities and friends. We can't have everything. It's difficult to decide what we really want.

In these quiet times of meditation, we can learn to listen to the inner voice that guides us to satisfying choices. However we understand the spiritual part of our lives, it can give us direction and a basis for making decisions.

May the choices I make today enhance the quality of my life and my recovery.

*Help is available — we don't have
to go it alone.*

Together we can do it: we can recover. Eating
disorders are habits of loneliness and isolation. To
get well we need help, and that help is always
available.

Those of us who belong to a Twelve Step support group have a list of phone numbers. We
know we can call people who will be there for us.
We go to meetings and share. We find that other
people have similar problems, and we stop feeling
lonely and isolated.

Some of us are in therapy, some of us have
strong family support systems, some of us have
friends and colleagues we can talk to when the going gets rough.

We can get help through our spiritual center.
We may define it in various ways, but when we
become aware of this center, we have an ever
present source of support.

*I will spend some quiet time today paying atten-
tion to the help that comes from my spiritual
center.*

• J A N U A R Y 6 •

The present is our power point.

We cannot change the past, nor can we control
the future. What we can do is become fully alive
to the challenge of this moment.

For those of us who tend to react to stress by
overeating, undereating, or bingeing and purging, the primary challenge of each moment is to
maintain abstinence from compulsive behavior
with regard to food. As long as we are not tied by
compulsion, we are free to respond with strength
and creativity to the reality of the present.

We have choices. We can choose new
responses to old situations. We can learn to recognize our true needs and choose positive ways of
satisfying them. We can select courses of action
that promote emotional and spiritual growth. We
can choose recovery — now — this moment.

*Today, I will use the power of the present — my
Higher Power is always now.*

Why not heed that gentle nudge?

Inner promptings — we can listen to them, or we can allow them to be drowned out by our busy routines, our habits, and our ways of thinking. The voice of creativity is often a quiet one. It may suggest a new way of operating that goes against our preconceived ideas.

Suppose angry words have been spoken. We feel uncomfortable. Underneath our discomfort is an urge to say something that could begin the process of reconciliation, but pride says no. Can we heed the inner urge and take a chance on making peace? Or suppose we haven't heard from a friend for a long time, but we feel it's the other person's turn to call. Do we respond to the inner nudge to make contact?

There are many ways we can heed our inner voice: We can trust our hunches about new activities we'd like to try, people we'd like to get to know, and thoughtful ways of helping our friends. We can be willing to risk ourselves and our schedules in the interest of growth.

I will respond today to the gentle nudges that enrich my recovery.

*Life seems to flow better when we
don't try to control it.*

When we were addicted to excess food or to
dieting, control was a key issue. We tried all sorts
of ways to control what we ate and how much we
weighed. We probably tried to control a lot of
other things, too, such as how the significant people in our lives behaved toward us, how co-
workers did their job, and what the weather fore-
cast would be for the next week.

A vital part of recovery is learning to accept the
things we cannot change. Those of us who work
a Twelve Step program accept our powerlessness
over people, places, and things, as well as over
compulsive eating and dieting. We come to believe that letting a Higher Power be in charge of
life in general and us in particular is the way to
sanity and serenity.

None of us has to believe this. Many of us are
skeptical at first. What we do is give the method
a try, one day at a time. Reports are that it works.
Experience shows that giving up the illusion of
control sets us free to enjoy what each day brings.

*Today, I will aim to follow my food plan and let
life happen.*

We can be our own best caretakers.

We may not have had the best parenting. Since parents are human, they have their own problems and aren't always able to give us what we need. We may look to friends, spouses, lovers, even to our own children to make up for the deficiency. But, as adults, we cannot realistically expect someone else to take care of us.

We can learn to listen to what our inner child is saying. We can heed the cues we receive from our body — a headache, a stiff neck, inappropriate hunger — that may indicate stress. Understanding and respecting our limits, we can learn to say no to what might jeopardize our serenity and well-being.

Even though we are no longer dependent children, we still need care and attention, and we are responsible for seeing that our needs are met. Although our problems may very well have their roots in a dysfunctional family situation, it is what we do now that counts. By taking care of ourselves and being convinced we deserve to have what we need, we act as responsible adults and stay out of the trap of dependency.

Today, I will give myself the care and attention I need.

Enthusiasm is contagious.

We get a real lift when we're around someone who is positive and enthusiastic. We seem to share a natural high with one another. If we gravitate toward people who make a habit of keeping their spirits up, we will "catch" their enthusiasm and be able to pass it along to those with whom we come in contact.

And we will undoubtedly pick up pointers on how to generate our own enthusiasm, starting with maintaining a healthy body. Abstinence generates enthusiasm. So do the Twelve Steps. Being released from the food and diet obsession goes a long way toward raising our spirits. So does getting rid of excess emotional baggage from the past, in the form of unnecessary guilt, fear, anger, and resentment.

The acceptance we receive from our friends in the program and from a Higher Power helps us feel confident and good about ourselves. With increased self-esteem comes increased enthusiasm, which spills over into all our activities and relationships.

I will try hard to be around enthusiastic people today and pass their enthusiasm along.

Impressive results come from small beginnings.

Do you remember your first abstinent day? You made a start on a new life. You probably worried that you might not be able to have another day of abstinence, but, with luck, someone reminded you to be concerned only with one day at a time, sometimes one hour at a time.

We are free to section our days and our accomplishments into small, manageable units. Books are written word by word and read sentence by sentence. Mountains are climbed step by step. A smile and a handshake can be the beginning of a lifelong friendship, and a casual conversation can launch a career.

Day by day, we build our recovery. We build it with the decisions we make, the people with whom we associate, the food we buy and prepare. We build it with the books we read, the way we spend our time, the care we give our body, the commitment we make to a Higher Power.

The beginning we make today is never insignificant or unimportant; it is the foundation of our future.

My new life continues to evolve, one day at a time.

Follow your bliss.

What is your heart's desire? Perhaps you are afraid to identify and go after it. Perhaps you think you won't be able to have it for some reason.

Those of us who were binge eaters may have thought that food was our heart's desire. But was it? We need to ask ourselves was it food, or was food a substitute for what we wanted but thought we couldn't or shouldn't have? Those of us who starved ourselves or who purged possibly thought that a socially acceptable body pointed the way to bliss. But did it? We need to ask ourselves if we thought that having a perfect body was the only way we would be acceptable — to ourselves as well as to others.

We know now that overeating is not bliss. Starvation and purging are not bliss either. We now have the opportunity to pursue our desires until we discover what brings happiness. Our search has led us to the Steps, and the Steps point to a spiritual reality that can illuminate our journey.

Abstinence clears away the depression and inertia that prevented us from identifying and going after our deepest heart's desire. We can follow our bliss.

I can be happy today.

*A mark of maturity is our ability to
live with ambiguity.*

One of the common characteristics shared by
many of us who have eating disorders is the tendency to view life by means of polarities. We
think in rigid terms of black and white, all or nothing, one extreme or the other. Then we find ourselves loving and hating someone, or pulled in
two different directions, and we have trouble fit-
ting our feelings into our rigid system of thought.

Growing up — and recovering — expand our
comfort level so we are better able to accept life's
paradoxes. The fact is that reality frequently de-
fies our attempts to categorize and sort it into
neatly labeled packages. We learn to live with
conflicting feelings, with situations where our
role seems murky rather than clear-cut.

With maturity, we have a deeper understanding
of both ourselves and others, which softens our
edges and helps us judge less and empathize
more. In humility we accept our limitations, and
in faith we leave what we do not understand to
the grace of a power greater than ourselves.

*Today, I will stretch my tolerance for life's
ambiguities.*

Mind and body fit together.

Being uncomfortable with one's body goes along with having an eating disorder. Many of us tried to ignore our bodies and lived in our minds. We fled to a fantasy world. Awareness of our bodies was mainly negative — we criticized them as too fat. Sometimes our body image was distorted — we considered ourselves fatter than we actually were. Declaring war on our bodies, we neglected their needs.

As we recover, we reclaim our bodies. We see ourselves more realistically. We become aware of the interrelationship between mind and body. We come to realize that if our physical needs are not met, we will not be emotionally healthy.

Accepting the things we cannot change includes accepting our individual body type and structure, as well as our need for exercise, rest, sex, and food. When our bodies are properly cared for, our minds function properly too. Becoming whole means integrating both mind and body.

Today, I will be aware of living in my body as well as my mind.

Abstinence is freedom.

Because we are abstinent today, we are free to do and enjoy the good things that come our way, and we are equipped to deal with our share of life's inevitable problems.

Joining a program for people with eating disorders gives us tools to use and a structure to follow on our journey out of compulsion into freedom. If we begin to get bored with the mechanics of our program — such as food plans — we need to remember what it was like before abstinence. Then, we were not free.

I am grateful to wake up in the morning alive and alert and free of the after-effects of a binge. I'm grateful to go through the day ready for work, play, problems, and challenges. I remember what it was like for me before abstinence, and I do not want to go back to that place. I am grateful for freedom.

May I stay abstinent and free today.

How deep is the hunger?

Our hunger may be deeper than we think. It may be that no amount of steak and potatoes or cheesecake will fill us up. It may even be that piles of money and countless love affairs won't do it, either. What's left to try? Drugs? A new wardrobe? A bigger house? A better job?

If being hungry goes along with being alive, then it stands to reason that somewhere life holds for us the experiences and relationships that will satisfy that hunger. It just may be that we've been looking in the wrong places.

What are the right places? It may be we are hungry for a hug or for words of understanding. We need to look for ways to feel useful, to have a sense of accomplishment. We need to look for ways to love and be loved. Our hunger has many levels. The deeper we go, the more fully we encounter our spiritual dimension.

Experiencing the depths of my hunger can help me discover how to feed my spirit.

*We grow by doing what's hard to
do.*

Avoiding issues went along with our eating disorder. We tended to sidestep what was uncomfortable to face. Rather than make decisions and take action, we often focused on food and diets. "When I reach goal weight, I'll deal with my other problems — maybe by that time they'll go away."

Recovery challenges us to confront and cope with whatever needs our attention. Each time we do so we become stronger. Maybe we need to do a house-cleaning project. Maybe we need to be more assertive with a boss or co-worker. Maybe we need to move out of a harmful relationship.

Bingeing or starving are no longer options. Using the tools of our program, we deal directly with the real issues. Although the task may seem difficult, we have help and support. With the help of our Higher Power, we will not be given more than we can handle.

I will accept today's challenges to grow.

How's your spiritual energy today?

We come to the Twelve Step program from a variety of spiritual traditions, or with no spiritual rooting at all. Even though some of us come with no formal affiliation, we all recognize the need for help from some source beyond ourselves, since we haven't been able to manage our eating disorder on our own.

The spiritual part of our program offers us a way to raise our level of spiritual energy, which is what will see us through to long-term recovery. Physical energy, emotional energy, and spiritual energy — we cannot separate them, since they all work together.

How do we nurture the spirit? We can participate regularly in religious services, set aside time for daily prayer and meditation, read, listen to music, seek the company of people who inspire us, appreciate the beauty of nature, be of service to someone else. In whatever we do, we can be aware of our relationship with a Power greater than ourselves and our spiritual interconnection with each other.

I will draw on the inexhaustible supply of spiritual energy that is available to me today and always.

When we let go of the idea of owner-ship, the world is ours to enjoy.

How easy it is to get tangled up in the desire to possess and acquire! For some of us, food represented all the things we thought we wanted but didn't have. Our binges, however, left us full of remorse and chronically unsatisfied. Others of us were obsessed with having the perfect shape, and no matter how much we dieted we were never thin enough, or so we thought.

Having to own, having to control — when we get caught up in these compulsions, nothing is ever enough.

What a relief it is to let go, to focus on enjoying rather than possessing and controlling. We can enjoy a sunset, a brisk or leisurely walk, a child, a friend, the satisfaction of a job well done. We can enjoy all of these things and much more as long as we do not think we must own or possess them or control how and when they will be a part of our lives.

What gifts does today bring for my enjoyment? I will allow them to move freely in and out of my life.

*Time and energy — how do we use
them?*

Do you find yourself wishing for more than
twenty-four hours in your day and more energy
to fill them? Certainly, time and energy are among
our most precious gifts. Without them, very little
would be possible.

How much time and energy did your eating disorder require? For most of us, the answer is "too
much." We no longer need to spend large blocks
of time thinking about food, planning a binge,
having it, and recovering from it. We no longer
need to drag ourselves around on the dangerously
low level of energy produced by self-starvation.

Even though recovery gives us time and energy
we did not have before, these precious gifts are
limited. Every day, the way we use these gifts de-
fines the new person we are becoming. Are we
learning to say yes to what enhances our growth
and no to what impedes it? Are we willing to let
our priorities be directed by a Higher Power?

*May I have the wisdom to know how I want to
spend my time and energy today.*

*Recognizing a dead end clears the
way for positive change.*

Seeking psychic income from food is a dead
end. No matter how good the food is or how
much we eat, that route cannot provide adequate
emotional nurturing. Bingeing doesn't solve
problems; it creates them. So do compulsive exercise and compulsive dieting. These are all dead
ends, sometimes literally.

Some of the relationships we become involved
in are also dead ends, because instead of meeting
our needs and desires, they bring us more negative returns than positive ones.

Dead ends are time consuming: Pursuing them
prevents us from moving along a path that leads
us where we want to go. They are also energy consuming: At best they are disappointing, and at
worst they are destructive or even fatal.

As we work our way through the Twelve Steps,
we become increasingly able to recognize these
futile courses of action for what they are. We also
find the power to change direction.

Today, I seek the wisdom to avoid dead ends.

What we give comes back to us.

Those of us who are part of a Twelve Step program are learning that we are responsible for our actions and reactions to other people. We are learning that we cannot control and change others, but we can change ourselves.

If we project hostility, hostility will come back to us. If we give love and acceptance, we will get them back — if not immediately, then eventually.

As we change our behavior, other people's reactions to us also change. If we want positive relationships in the present, we must be willing to let go of old hurts and resentments.

Recovery means moving away from any bitterness lingering from the past. When we do our amends Steps, we become increasingly free from old hurts and resentments. We can turn them over to a Higher Power and decide today to treat other people the way we'd like them to treat us.

How many times today can I give what I'd like to receive?

Nothing ventured, nothing gained.

We pray for "courage to change the things we can." Change requires giving up familiar old ways to try something new. Even though the old ways brought us pain, they were known. Changing them for new ones feels risky; it could lead to pleasure . . . or to even more pain.

But if we don't try, we'll never know whether we can handle a new job, go back to school, work out a new relationship, or breathe new life into an old one. To try something new, we have to be willing to take risks and be vulnerable. We have to accept the responsibility and the consequences if our venture does not proceed as we had hoped it would.

Perhaps our eating disorder was a way of avoiding risk. Rather than take the chance of failing at something we wanted to do or being rejected by someone to whom we offered our friendship, we focused on food. Are we ready, now, to take risks for something we really want?

Today, I can take a small risk in the interest of enriching my life.

*The closer we get to a Higher Power,
the better the pieces of our life seem
to fit together.*

Because we could not manage our eating disorder by ourself, we became willing to entertain the idea of trusting a Higher Power. Out of desperation came a new way of life, infinitely better than our old way, which was built on the illusion of self-sufficiency.

It's amazing how events unfold when we make a conscious decision to turn our will and our life over to the God of our understanding. The people we need appear on our path, the right challenges come along as we are ready for them, and looking back we see how everything fits into place.

This is not an unusual experience for those of us in Twelve Step programs — it is one of the promises. In the words of the Big Book, "We will suddenly realize that God is doing for us what we could not do for ourselves."

May I allow my Higher Power to work for me today.

The mud settles when we clarify our priorities.

There are times when we ask ourselves what's really important to us. It might be doing well in school, losing twenty pounds, making money, developing a relationship, or buying a house. Many projects and possibilities clamor for our attention. Unless we have a method of sorting them out, we may find ourselves mired in confusion and frustration.

First things first is what the program suggests. But what *is* first? For those of us who have suffered from out-of-control, addictive behavior, recovery is first. Our other priorities follow from our primary commitment to recovery. We pursue what enhances it, and we avoid what threatens it. For many of us, freedom from compulsive behavior becomes possible as we develop a relationship with a Higher Power.

To be effective, priorities need to come from within rather than be imposed from without. That means listening to our inner voice. As we listen quietly, the mud settles and our confusion clears.

I will determine my priorities for today and avoid confusion.

*What is your spiritual temperature
today?*

Are there some mornings when your waking
thought is "I can't face another day"? Before we
were recovering, days like this were likely to send
us off on a binge or into compulsive restricting.

We have come to believe we are given a daily
reprieve from self-destructive behavior, a daily
reprieve contingent on our spiritual condition.
Maintaining a healthy spiritual condition means
using the tools of our program — reading the literature, going to meetings, spending time each day
in quiet meditation, being of service to other people, working the Twelve Steps.

When our spiritual temperature is not a healthy
one, there are ways to get back in touch with a
Higher Power. Probably the simplest and most effective way is to take a few moments to be still and
listen to the inner voice that can tell us what's
wrong and suggest a possible solution.

*If my spiritual temperature is not healthy today,
it's time to still myself and ask for direction from
my Higher Power.*

We seek progress, not perfection.

It would be nice if we could follow our food plan perfectly every day, accomplish everything on our schedule efficiently, and have flawless interpersonal relationships. It would be, but it's an unrealistic expectation.

Since we are human, we will make mistakes — in our work, our dealings with other people, and our choices about food. If we're prepared to forgive ourselves and start again, a minor slip need not become a major relapse.

If we hurt someone, we can promptly make amends to the best of our ability. If we let ourselves down by slipping back into old habits, we can gently correct our course without feeling that we have failed.

We are learning. Each time we choose to eat what our bodies require for good nutrition, each time we refrain from hurtful behavior to ourselves or others, each time we nourish our minds and hearts with interesting and rewarding activities, we make progress.

Today, I will concentrate on taking one step forward, however small.

There is no finish line.

Picture a runner going around a lake. The course doesn't end. It continues as long as the runner wants to run, and the joy is in the experience of running, not in arriving at a specific destination.

As soon as we reach one goal, another appears further ahead. As long as we are alive, we never exhaust our opportunities for growth. This is as it should be, since life is a process, a journey.

We continue to set goals for ourselves, but we recognize them for what they are — markers along the way. We no longer have a compulsion to reach a certain marker at a certain time. If our course changes direction, we may miss some markers entirely, but that's okay. We continue the journey, knowing that a Higher Power is in charge and will show us the course to follow each day.

Today, I will enjoy the journey and let my Higher Power take care of the destination.

*If food is a problem, so is something
else.*

When we are tempted to try to feel better by
overeating or undereating, we need to ask ourselves some questions. "What is really bothering
me? What can I do to relieve the stress in a healthy
way? How can I avoid a slip and turn my discomfort into a positive learning experience?"

When abstinence feels shaky, we can learn to
listen to our inner discomfort. "Am I angry?
Afraid? Worried? Depressed?" We know that, in
the long run, bingeing will not help, nor will purging or starving.

The Twelve Steps give us a way of coping with
the problems we identify. So do the friends we
make when we join a support group. So do the insights that come when we listen to our inner
voice. So does our Higher Power.

*Today, instead of listening to my addiction, may
I listen to my feelings and to the program for answers to my problems.*

*The answers may be simple, but
they're not always easy.*

We pray for the serenity to accept the things we
cannot change, courage to change the things we
can, and wisdom to know the difference. Even
when we know the difference, accepting and
changing may not be easy to do.

There may be "givens" in our current situation
that we don't like but must live with. We may be
faced with the serious illness of a family member.
Or, we may realize that it's necessary to relocate
to keep our job.

We may need to change some things — to leave
unfulfilling jobs or to arrange to spend more time
with our family.

The answers to our problems may be simple —
accept this, change that — but when it comes to
implementing these answers, we may need help.
That's when we call on the inner strength we
build each day during our times of prayer and
meditation.

---

*Today, I will seek a renewed supply of serenity,
courage, and wisdom.*

Sharing decreases our pain and increases our joy.

Overeating was lonely. So was compulsive dieting. We tried to find in food what we were afraid to ask for from other people. Or we tried to make ourselves "perfectly thin" so that others would accept and admire us.

We don't have to do either of these things anymore. We can reach out to other people. We can share our pain and our joy instead of keeping them locked inside. Friends make us feel better than food ever did. We learn that we have much to give and that we can be loved and accepted according to how well we give of ourselves, not for how much we weigh.

Burdens shared become lighter. Joys shared are multiplied. When we are willing to risk disclosure to another person, the rewards can be great. Our Higher Power does not intend us to be alone. Each day brings new opportunities to strengthen and deepen our links to those around us.

Today, I will risk sharing a part of myself with someone else. I will not hide in food or diets.

February

Honesty is a prerequisite for
spiritual growth.

One measure of our growth through a Twelve Step program is how honest we are with ourselves and others. Secrets and denial were part of our illness. Identifying and sharing our true thoughts and feelings promote recovery.

We may have been afraid to honestly face ourselves, but now we have the example and support of others who have found that the Twelve Steps work when we work them. Honesty may threaten the status quo. But in the long run it is the only solid foundation for communication with other people, and the only way we become acquainted with our inner self.

Wherever we're going, we must start where we are and as we are. Deception and pretense block our progress. When we present ourselves truthfully, even at the risk of saying something someone else may not want to hear, we open the door to growth and better understanding.

My emerging self is always on the side of honesty.
May I risk being true to it today.

Every end is a new beginning.

Graduating. Moving. Breaking up a relation-ship. Finishing a project. Changing jobs. Each of these is an ending, and each marks the beginning of a new stage of our journey through life.

We think of endings as sad, and they often are. The wrench of leaving the loved and familiar can be felt as both physical and emotional pain. But if we do not leave the old, we cannot move on to the new. One door shuts, and another opens.

We take our experience and knowledge from the past with us as we move into the future. They are not lost but transformed.

Now that we are facing problems squarely in-stead of hiding out in food and diets, our aware-ness sharpens to the pain of endings and the excitement and anxiety of new beginnings. If we need help with these feelings, we know it is avail-able from a Power greater than ourselves.

I will trust my Higher Power to see me through each ending to a new beginning, one day at a time.

• FEBRUARY 3 •

*If we search with sincerity, answers
will appear.*

We want to solve our problems, become better
people, and realize our potential. The dissatisfaction with our faults and weaknesses prompts us to
seek help — from books, our friends, professional
counselors, and support groups.

If we keep looking and asking and following
our inner promptings, we will find the help we
seek. For many of us, joining a Twelve Step program created a new dimension in our quest for
meaningful answers. We have a growing conviction that when we are ready, answers will appear.

*May I continue my quest to understand. May my
actions today reflect sincerity of purpose and
courage to change the things I can.*

*What do you do when you want to
do it all?*

Our options open a universe of possibilities to us, but choosing between them is sometimes overwhelming. For example, the prospect of a free day — one that we can structure largely according to our personal preference — can fill us with purposefulness, excitement, or peace . . . or with anxiety and panic.

In our compulsiveness, some of us tend to fall apart without external structures such as lengthy "to-do" lists and exhausting social schedules. In the past, when I couldn't decide what to do with free time, I often turned to food. Bingeing took care of the problem of how to spend the day. There was soon no more day to spend!

Now I choose other activities, but I need to be selective, saying yes to some and no to others. That's where I need to rely on the inner sense of direction that develops through contact with my Higher Power.

———————————

*I can't do it all. I will rely on my Higher Power to
show me what's most important today.*

*We sell ourselves short if the scale is
our primary source of approval.*

People with eating disorders spend lots of time
getting on and off the scale. When we are obsessed with reaching and maintaining a specific
weight, the moving indicator on the scale becomes our judge. Weight okay: we feel good.
Weight not okay: we feel terrible.

In recovery, we focus on eating the right type
and amount of food, and we let our weight take
care of itself. We concentrate on following a path
toward emotional and spiritual growth that allows us to feel good about ourselves. We have
value; we have gifts to give; our self-worth is not
dependent on what the scale reports.

As our recovery progresses, we cultivate
friends among those who value us for our inner
assets rather than our outward appearance. We
are free to become who we are intended to be,
and we enjoy the process of self-discovery. True
self-esteem comes from within, rather than from
numbers on a scale.

*Whatever my weight today, I am a worthwhile
person with valuable contributions to make to
those around me.*

Life is more than abstinence.

Abstinence is just the beginning of recovery. It's true that without a commitment to eat moderate, healthy meals each day, we run the risk of lapsing into our eating disorder, so abstinence is a very necessary beginning. But much more can be gained from our new life in the program.

Most of us have tried many diets and counted many calories. Because that route did not work for us, we became willing to consider the Twelve Step program, a method that deals with much more than the food we do or do not eat.

Abstinence frees us from our obsessive preoccupation with food and diets so that we can get involved with what was missing in our lives. Once we've made our food plan for the day, we can put that issue to rest and think about love, work, play, hobbies, other people. Motivating our interest and enthusiasm is the spiritual power that comes from the God of our understanding.

Today, I will select from the broad range of possibilities that life offers and abstinence makes possible.

Some of the best things in life happen slowly.

It takes time, lots of time, for a friendship to fully develop. Surely, one of life's most satisfying experiences is watching a child grow from infancy to adulthood. Building a house takes time. So does becoming established in a career, learning to play a good game of tennis, and nurturing a relationship with a Higher Power.

Recovering from an eating disorder takes time. We need to be patient with ourselves if progress is not as rapid as we would like. Undoubtedly, our problems with food did not spring up overnight, and it is not likely that they will vanish instantly either.

With time and patience, we can learn to give food its proper place in our lives as nourishment for our bodies. Slowly our abstinence becomes solid, and slowly our minds and hearts are fed by satisfying relationships, work, and activities.

Perhaps I can be more patient with my recovery today than I was yesterday.

*Recovery teaches us to love who we
are.*

I am not finished. I am growing, changing, and evolving. Nevertheless, I like myself today. I am aware of possibilities for improvement, but I don't want to be anyone else. I have become comfortable with and accepting of who I am. Looking back on some of the things I have done that proved to be poor ideas, I can understand why I acted as I did. I can forgive my mistakes and move on to try again.

First, we accept the things we cannot change — things such as our height, body build, eye color, family of origin, aptitudes, and conditioning. Then, we go beyond acceptance to the realization that these characteristics are part of what makes us special. Even our less desirable attributes, such as our tendency to overeat or undereat, are part of who we are. Gently and lovingly, we can create for ourselves the kind of supportive environment that will allow us to function at our best. Each time we make and follow a food plan that fills our individual needs, we are actively loving who we are.

Today, I'm glad to be me.

Listening feeds the spirit.

If we give each other our full attention and really listen, we can't help but become closer. I am nourished by your attention, as you are by mine.

Often our attention is anything but focused: we ask a question but fail to listen to the answer. We half listen to the other person, at the same time thinking about what we will say next, or about something extraneous to the conversation.

Genuine communication includes pauses and silences — times when we let ourselves feel the impact of our friend's words, reflect deeply on them, and frame our answers carefully before speaking. In this exchange, we learn, share, receive, and give. We are participants in a dialogue of mind, heart, and spirit.

Today, I will focus my attention fully on someone's words, if only for a few minutes. I will seek to nourish and be nourished.

Food does not fix relationships.

Negative feelings and resentments have a way of resurfacing even when we think we've moved beyond them. Since these feelings are uncomfortable, we look for ways to get rid of them. Many of us tried to stuff them down with food, and some of us tried to starve them away.

Attempting to ignore anger and resentment doesn't work very well. What we need is a way of mending relationships so that negative feelings do not become excuses to abuse food and our bodies.

Instead of trying to get even with someone we feel has mistreated us, and instead of misusing food in an effort to feel better, we have new options. We can ask for help from a Higher Power. We can examine our attitudes and behavior and keep making amends promptly. We can seek help from a friend or counselor. We can talk to the other person about ways to resolve the conflict. Finally, when we have done everything we can do, we can let go and let God.

What I can't fix today, I can turn over.

Positive or negative — the choice is ours.

Every day we make a choice: we focus on the positive or on the negative. Today, for instance, we can fix our attention on the cold weather, or we can be thankful for the diversity of the seasons. We can wake up grumbling about having to go to work, or we can wake in gratitude that we are able to earn a living.

Some things will always concern us — paying the bills, raising the children, fixing the roof, staying healthy, getting along with those we love, planning for the future. But if this is all we think about, we are missing the sense of deep appreciation that makes us feel full and satisfied with life's gifts.

Let's take a moment today to begin to make a list of the positive, starting with the fact that we're alive and abstinent.

May I remember today that life is a gift.

*A good way to start the day is by
saying thank-you.*

First of all, we can be thankful for the gift of life. Then, we can think about our other blessings, especially those that go along with recovery.

With abstinence goes the ability to wake up in the morning clearheaded, feeling good, and ready to tackle the day's challenges. We experience a new appreciation for the beauty of nature and for the friendliness and kindness we encounter among those whose lives we touch. Saying thank-you for opportunities to love and work keeps us from taking these good things for granted and helps us feel full instead of empty.

As the day progresses, we may get busy, preoccupied with problems, and tired. But when we take time to set a tone of gratitude at the beginning of the day, we have a base to come back to for refreshment. The more times we say thank-you, the more our serenity expands.

I will say thank-you for today's gifts.

*Once we clear a hurdle, it doesn't
seem so high.*

Anything — from cleaning the house, to doing
a Fourth Step inventory, to taking the bar exam,
to apologizing for a mistake — can be a hurdle.
What seems to me to be a Herculean task may
sound easy to you. But in my mind it's a hurdle,
and, until I clear it, I will probably experience
some degree of anxiety.

Sometimes we can break a big task into small
pieces and tackle the job a piece at a time. If the
task is complex, sometimes it's best if we work on
it gradually, focusing only on what needs to be
done today, one day at a time. Often when we
look back on the ordeal, we realize that we had
the help of a Higher Power and that clearing the
hurdle wasn't all that tough. And, even if it was
tough, once we've cleared a high hurdle, we realize that it probably won't be so hard to clear the
next time.

*May I remember that the tasks and events that
loom large today will probably be easier once I
develop an action plan and get started.*

Today's actions are tomorrow's memories.

This day will not come again. Its opportunities are unique. I have been given these twenty-four hours to spend working, communicating, loving, giving, exercising, playing, eating, learning, sleeping, meditating, enjoying.

How I treat a friend, what kind of support I give to my family, how conscientiously I do my job — what I do today will be remembered tomorrow by the people involved. I will remember, too, and I want my memories to be good ones.

I am learning to be responsible for my actions. I pray for guidance. I trust that what I do today will fit into the pattern that is my life. Even though I can't see the entire design of my life now, I believe that a pattern exists and that it is unfolding day by day.

May my actions today build good memories for tomorrow.

As we learn to share what we have,
we begin to have enough.

The world is a treasure house, and we each have a key. The key is what we give to other people. We give our time, our talents, our material goods — and as we give, we also receive.

We may have been afraid that we didn't have *anything* to give, or that what we gave wouldn't be good enough. That could be one reason we began compulsive eating. Or, we may have started dieting obsessively in search of the physical perfection we thought would make us acceptable to ourselves and other people.

Through the program, we gain confidence in the wealth we have to share. We can give a smile, words of encouragement and affirmation, thoughtful criticism, a few hours of baby-sitting, a hug, or a touch. We can give by telling others what means most to us. Giving makes us feel rich.

What will I share and give today?

*It's often easier to know what we
need to do than to do it.*

We each have our own definition of abstinence. We know what we need to eat to feel good
and be healthy. We know what substances, activities, and people are hazardous to our well-being.
We know, but sometimes we don't act on our
knowledge.

The beauty of our program is that we can keep
trying. We can make mistakes, get into trouble,
come back to our source of strength, and try
again. Each day we refine our knowledge of what
works for us and what doesn't. Every Twelve Step
meeting we attend reinforces our understanding
of the problem and the solution. Others who are
walking the same path give us the benefit of their
experience.

If we are committed to recovery, we will act as
well as understand. We will do the necessary
work and take the Steps leading to the spiritual
awakening that gives our life direction and
fulfillment.

*Today, I will do those things that strengthen my
recovery.*

We can't foresee the outcome of the journey, but we can take the next step.

Many of us wonder where our lives are going. We question whether we will have enough money to do what we want, where our careers are going, or if it's possible for us to have an intimate relationship with someone.

Many possibilities are open to us. We often don't know which path to take or what will result from the choices we make.

Although we do not know our destination in advance, we can learn to trust a Higher Power for direction and purpose. When we earnestly seek to know and do our Higher Power's will, the answers to our questions appear when we are ready to receive them.

Today I will trust that my Higher Power will show me the next step on my journey, as well as my destination.

Recovery never stops — there's always room for growth.

When is it over? When do we say, "Okay, now I'm well, so I can sit back and be recovered"?

Fortunately, we never arrive at that point. There is no finish line for emotional and spiritual growth. As human beings, we are continually evolving and becoming — getting better. Our lives are not static. We are constantly confronted with new challenges, which stretch us to further develop our potential. In order not to slip back, we must continue to move forward.

And that's what makes life interesting and exciting. Now that we are awake and aware, we can see possibilities that probably never occurred to us when we were controlled by our eating disorder. One stage leads to another in our development as caring, sensitive, productive individuals. We can always learn to be more tolerant, humble, gracious, sincere, loving, courageous, generous, honest, and integrated. Growth is what recovery is all about.

May I continue to work on recovering.

Boredom is optional.

For many of us, being obsessed with food and diets was connected to boredom. Food and diets themselves became boring. Having unstructured time or being in what we considered a dull situation triggered our compulsive patterns. Now that we are more aware of options and possibilities, we can become more interested and less bored.

If we are alert and alive to the reality of the present, we need never be bored. It's when we close ourselves off from the natural stimulation that comes from the environment, from others, and from within that we think there's nothing interesting going on. The fact is, there's plenty going on; we're just not fully aware of it.

When we find ourselves feeling bored, we should first ascertain that fatigue or anxiety is not masquerading as lack of interest. If not, then we can give ourselves permission to think about or do or plan something that sparks our enthusiasm. This will require paying close attention to our internal cues. The solution to boredom may be as simple as giving undivided attention to our own thoughts, feelings, and sensations.

If I am bored today, I may need to learn more about myself.

*If your telephone doesn't ring, pick
it up and call someone.*

Waiting for the phone to ring puts us in the position of being reactive rather than proactive. We are allowing someone else to determine our mood. We are passively waiting for another person to make the first move.

How much better we feel when we become willing to reach out ourselves! Each day, we probably come in contact with many people who would like our attention and appreciation. Opportunities abound to get involved in community groups and worthwhile causes. Instead of sitting around waiting to be fed emotionally, we need to give our care and concern to those whose lives we touch.

In the process of nurturing, we are nurtured. Our gifts to one another can be as simple as a phone call to a person we haven't seen at a meeting for some time, or to an old friend with whom we've lost touch. We are recovering. We have experience, strength, and hope to share.

I will make time to call someone today.

Quality is part of having enough.

Mere quantity does not satisfy — ask anyone who binges. Quantities of food, of things, of love affairs, of achievements do not by themselves fill our emptiness. We need quality as well, if we are to feel we have enough.

Food satisfies us when we eat the right amount of what we need nutritionally. "Empty" calories leave us craving more. Our physical hunger can be satisfied as long as we do not try to use food to fill emotional and spiritual needs. For those needs, we require both quality experiences and relationships.

·One deep relationship does more for us than a dozen superficial ones. A job well done produces more satisfaction than completing several jobs in a slipshod fashion. A few quiet moments spent reflecting on a source of power greater than ourselves is more rewarding than hours of noisy "entertainment." As we deepen our recovery, we learn what satisfies.

Today, I will focus on the quality of what I take in and give out.

Trying new things keeps us alive
and growing.

I know a man who learned to ski at age sixty-six and a woman who took up ballroom dancing as a grandmother. I also know people who probably haven't learned anything new in the last three years. I hope I'll be learning as long as I live.

An important part of recovery is breaking out of old ruts and doing something different, perhaps something we've wanted to do for a long time but never dared attempt. Our old ways of thinking are changing, we see new possibilities, and we gain confidence in our ability to accomplish our goals.

When we believe that a Higher Power accepts us just as we are, the pressure is off. We are free to experiment and find out what we enjoy. Our old fears of inadequacy begin to depart, and new situations no longer panic us. We may even go looking for challenges instead of dreading them. Life after abstinence is an adventure. We learn to welcome the unknown as an opportunity for growth.

Today, I will be open to growing by trying something new.

Other people can't meet our needs if we don't tell them what our needs are.

We need tenderness and caring from our families and friends. We need their acceptance, understanding, and support. Sometimes we need their criticism and forgiveness.

Whatever our needs are, other people will probably be involved in getting them met. If we expect those close to us to read our minds and know exactly what we want without being told, we will probably be disappointed. Being honest and candid about our needs and feelings is an important goal of recovery. Asking directly for what we want is one way to avoid using food to try to solve our problems. True, the other person may say no, but being able to make a reasonable request raises our self-esteem and opens the door to communication.

Today, I will take the risk of asking someone directly for something I want.

*It is unrealistic to expect a
permanent high.*

Recovery from an eating disorder does not guarantee a pink-cloud existence. We still have days when we wake up with a flat, "blah" feeling that persists in spite of efforts to shake it.

For most of us, searching for a high was part of our problem with food. Whether we got high from bingeing or from starving, we were trying to alter our mood. Now that we're in recovery, we can give ourselves permission to feel less than elated. We can remember how depressed we felt when our eating behavior was on the crazy side, and we can appreciate how much better our down days are now. Many of us agree that our worst days now are better than our best days then.

When our mood is less than exuberant, we can accept that fact without trying to manipulate our feelings with food. We no longer strive to be perpetually up. Level is fine, and downs can be tolerated with the help of our expanding inner resources.

I don't expect to be high all day today. I will let my moods ebb and flow freely.

If food isn't the answer, what is?

We know what we don't want to do: we don't want to be trapped in compulsive patterns of behavior that are harmful and that prevent us from functioning at our best. Knowing this is a big step forward in our recovery, but it isn't everything. We still need to figure out what we do want to do.

When we're eating normally and not trying to make food solve our problems, our real needs and desires eventually surface. When we're sincerely seeking to think and act in harmony with our inner self and with the God of our understanding, we begin to find answers that satisfy us in a way that food never did.

For me, the answers revolve around love and work. When I am functioning well in these areas, food is not a problem. When I look for direction from a Higher Power and do the best I can to follow that direction, both love and work are satisfying.

I am grateful to find answers to my deepest needs.

Recovery's challenge — learning to love.

Excess food won't make us happy. Neither will excess dieting. We need real, live people to satisfy our emotional hunger.

And they're all around us — in our families, at school, at work, in the community. First, we acknowledge that we need people: a box of cookies is no substitute for a friend and neither is a "perfect" day, when we restrict our eating to a single salad. Then, we take the risk of opening up, of becoming vulnerable, of giving time, care, and attention to someone else.

One of the nice things about loving is that we don't have to do it perfectly to reap benefits. Even a little love makes a big difference in how we feel.

Another nice thing about love is that through our Higher Power we have access to an inexhaustible supply. The more love we give away, the more we get back.

Learning to love invites my full attention. I may not do it perfectly, but today I can deepen my commitment to those whom I love.

*Allowing others their individuality
assures us of our own.*

If we don't want to be manipulated, then we must be careful to avoid trying to manipulate others. Manipulation doesn't work — it breeds resentment and retaliation, which we act on or stew over.

When we stop medicating ourselves with too much or too little food, we may try to get our needs met by using other people in a selfish, controlling way. This is harmful to us as well as to them.

The Twelve Step program teaches us to live and let live, to accept that those we love will make their own choices according to their inner needs. We can learn to respect those choices and the people who make them. As we permit others to be themselves, we also become free to develop our own individuality.

If I am tempted to try to control another person today, I will release both of us to my Higher Power's care.

An ordinary day can be extra-ordinarily nice.

Recognizing and enjoying the unspectacular pleasures of every day nourishes our spirits so that we do not crave an unnatural high. Small satisfactions, routine accomplishments, and simple pleasures make us feel good, when we take the time to appreciate them and when we're free from the addictive behaviors that spoil them.

Believe it or not, when we're eating reasonably, even cleaning the garage can be fun. But if we're not, nothing we do is likely to be truly pleasurable. Even the most ordinary abstinent day can be quite nice, especially when we remember to compare it with the days when our eating was out of control. We no longer have to seek great highs if we remember that what goes up must come down.

Abstinence puts us on an even keel physically, and the Steps keep us emotionally and spiritually balanced. When we are thus in equilibrium, the ordinary events in our daily lives take on a special luster.

I don't need fireworks today. Quiet satisfaction will be just fine.

*We can learn to reduce stress and
tension.*

Stress is part of being alive, and some of it is good for us. The right amount of positive stress challenges and motivates us to develop our potential. Without a certain amount of tension, we might lose our zest for life.

Too often, however, stress and tension build to the point where we feel their effects as negative instead of positive. In response, we may overeat, undereat, or binge and purge in an attempt to relieve our discomfort. When we become abstinent, we still must deal with stress. Sometimes we develop physical symptoms such as headaches, neckaches, and backaches.

Part of living abstinently is learning how to relax without using a substance such as a tranquilizer. Exercising, taking deep breaths, sitting quietly, practicing the relaxation response — all are ways to reduce tension. One of the best ways is to remember many times a day that we are cared for by a Higher Power.

*When I feel my teeth clenching today, I will draw
a deep breath and let my Higher Power take over.*

March

*Fear of commitment can be a road-
block to recovery.*

As we proceed along the path of recovery, we are invited to make commitments. If we're following a Twelve Step program, these commitments are not demanded of us, but they are strongly recommended by people who have traveled a similar path.

The commitments of our program include abstinence, working the Steps, going to meetings, and developing a relationship with a Higher Power. If we're afraid to devote ourselves to these, our progress may be blocked. In the process of overcoming our fears, we are able to move ahead to more solid and complete recovery.

As people become more important than food to our emotional health, we are invited to deepen and strengthen our commitments to those whose lives we touch. This can be frightening. Is it decreased control and increased vulnerability that we fear? We need to carefully consider our opportunities for growth-enhancing commitments and not be afraid to make ones that will advance our recovery.

*I pray for courage and wisdom to make and
maintain positive commitments.*

*Fears and doubts get smaller when
we talk about them.*

Our fears loom large when we keep them to
ourselves. Sometimes we not only keep them hidden from other people, we also keep them from
our own conscious awareness. All of us experience fear and doubt. Denying these feelings is
unhealthy; so is covering them up with compulsive overeating or dieting.

Each of us needs at least one person with whom
we can share our fears and doubts. When we talk
about them, they tend to shrink and are less likely
to overwhelm us. If no one is around to listen to
our fears and doubts, we can write about them as
a prelude to airing them with someone.

Sometimes our fears are justified. We should be
afraid of whatever threatens our recovery. Being
honest with another human being helps us sort
out the fears and doubts we should respect from
those we can relinquish and turn over to a Higher
Power.

*Today, I will make the decision to share my fears
and doubts with a trusted friend.*

*Recovery shifts our focus from the
outside to the inside.*

In the past, some of us weighed ourselves many
times a day, were intensely preoccupied with the
size of our bodies, and judged ourselves and
others by external standards.

Recovering alcoholics say, "My insides looked
at your outsides, and so I drank." Those of us who
are recovering from anorexia, bulimia, and
compulsive overeating understand what this
means. It means we need to build our self-esteem
on the lasting values of the Twelve Step program.
As we work on cultivating qualities such as honesty, courage, faith, love, and responsibility, we
will become less preoccupied with external
appearance.

If we judge others by how they look, we will
also judge ourselves in the same way, and we will
be unhappy because we seldom measure up to the
standards of perfection we set. Our program sets
new and different standards. We focus on who we
are inside, rather than on how we look.

---

*Today, I will move beyond superficial exteriors
and try to develop inner spiritual values as I
work my program.*

We can make a difference.

The people who cross our path today can benefit from our gifts. We can give a smile, words of encouragement, assistance with a project, an honest and caring response.

With abstinence from bingeing and dieting, we become more sensitive to those around us. We have more energy and attention to give to friends, family, co-workers, and even to the strangers with whom we interact.

By staying tuned to the forces of goodness, we can make a positive difference in the lives of other people. We can share our experience, strength, and hope — what works for us — and in the process receive new gifts. Service makes us strong.

How can I contribute to making today better for someone else?

*Our effectiveness comes from
within.*

Whatever we do, we will do it best when we are whole. Recovering from an eating disorder means knitting together the parts of ourselves that were separated and in conflict. We fought ourselves about what we ate, and our inner conflicts spilled over into our outward behavior.

When we give the warring elements within a chance to be heard and healed, we can stop fighting and get on with the business of living constructively. When we fill our bodies, minds, and hearts with the good things we need — rest, proper nutrition, satisfying work, loving and caring — our effectiveness grows.

We each have a unique contribution to make. The further we get from food addiction, the closer we come to being the effective, well-integrated person we are meant to be.

Today, I will take steps to become a more whole person.

We don't know what we can do
until we try.

Recovery may seem hard, but isn't the alternative worse? It is often difficult and painful to learn how to face our problems without resorting to some kind of food abuse. We may think that we can't do it.

The beauty of our program is that no matter how difficult it may seem to follow, we follow it for only twenty-four hours at a time. When we discover what we can do during one twenty-four-hour period, we are encouraged to try again the next day. Little by little, day by day, our confidence grows.

So, too, with other new ventures that our inner voice prompts us to try. At first, a new job, a move, or a new relationship may seem fraught with difficulty. As we reach out for help from our support system, and as we learn to trust our innate capabilities, we find ourselves doing things that once may have seemed impossible.

Today, I will make an effort to take one small step toward reaching one of my goals.

Good timing means learning to wait.

We might think our lives would be improved if all our desires were satisfied according to our timetable. That might be true, but instant gratification is not a realistic expectation. Sometimes that's just as well, since what we wanted yesterday may not be what we want today.

If we have snacked and binged compulsively in the past, we can learn to channel our appetite into a reasonable pattern of moderate meals. This means we have to wait to satisfy our hunger. If other impulsive behaviors have created problems for us, we can also learn to wait for the appropriate time to satisfy these needs and wants. Learning how to delay gratification is part of growing up. Some of us learn more slowly than others, but we all can do it!

One of the advantages of believing in a Higher Power is that we come to accept that our Higher Power's timetable is different from our own. Being willing to wait is easier when we trust that we will get what we need when we need it.

May my timing today come closer to my Higher Power's timing.

Trust your instincts.

One of the promises of the Twelve Step program is that "we will intuitively know how to handle situations that used to baffle us."* The Steps and abstinence work together to hone our intuition, making us better equipped to receive internal messages.

Can you believe that your inner self knows what you need today and can lead you in the direction you should move to fill those needs?

As children, we may not have been encouraged to trust our instincts. The grown-ups around us may have thought they knew better. When we don't trust our own judgment and inner promptings, we are cut off from valuable guidance.

True, we should seek information and advice, and we can profit from another's experience. But in the final analysis, we need to be able to make decisions and act according to our inner direction. The more we cultivate conscious contact with a Higher Power, the more reliable that direction is.

—————

As I recover, I am learning to trust my instincts.

*Alcoholics Anonymous (New York: Alcoholics Anonymous World Services, Inc., 1955), 84.

Change is a certainty.

There's no way any of us is going to travel from the cradle to the grave without experiencing change, lots of it. We can wear ourselves out trying to preserve the status quo, but we won't succeed. We are fated to be caught up in change — in ourselves, in others, and in our lives.

Even though we know that change is inevitable, and that without it there can be no growth, we still resist it. Perhaps this is because we fear the unknown and feel threatened by what is new. Fear of change can prevent us from taking advantage of promising opportunities. Resistance to what is new can keep us focused on past situations and on responses that won't work with our current reality.

By accepting changes in our lives — graduation, divorce, a new boss, the death of someone close, a promotion, children leaving home — we are able to function in the present and make the most of it.

I can cope with change today without turning to food or away from it.

*Our weaknesses bring us closer to
each other and to a Higher Power.*

Only by being wounded do we learn to seek
and find healing. Through our weaknesses we understand our need for help, empathize with the
suffering of another person, and become agents
of healing for each other.

As we journey toward health and wholeness,
we will undoubtedly experience difficulties and
setbacks. When we encounter these problems,
we can lament life's unfairness, or we can accept
our difficulties as challenges, using them to spur
us on to continued growth.

When we hurt, we can turn to a source of healing greater than ourselves. That power is within
each of us, and we can release it in each other.
Listening, caring, being there for those we love,
following examples of courage, believing that
how we respond makes a difference, converting
weakness to strength — these are the hallmarks of
recovery.

Today, I will let my weakness lead me to healing.

It's okay to have fun.

Although we're working hard on recovering, we can also have fun. In fact, we can have much more fun now than we did before we found the program. With the awakening of our spiritual self, life takes on new zest. We smile more and frown less.

We can give ourselves permission to enjoy whatever comes our way, as long as it does not threaten abstinence or serenity. Friends, food, the multitude of activities, experiences, and sensations that life presents to us each day: all these are to be enjoyed.

Fun and the food obsession were mutually exclusive. Now that we have the tools for recovery, we can expect more fun. Using the inventory and amends Steps, we can clear away any emotional debris from the past that may be hampering our enjoyment of the present. As we take ourselves less seriously, our sense of humor blossoms. Laughter delights and heals us.

I will let myself enjoy life and have some fun today.

Stop trying to control — start living.

I can't control you, you can't control me, and neither of us can completely control our environment. If we stopped trying, we'd become more free and spontaneous.

This is easier said than done, but the Twelve Steps show us the way. Though we are responsible for ourselves and our own behavior, we do not have the ability to force others to do what we would like them to. When we accept this, really accept it, we usually feel a great sense of relief.

Living spontaneously means responding to the reality of each moment instead of trying to make the course of events conform to our preconceived plan. We are free to initiate and respond; we are not free to control.

We can learn to accept that life will follow its own course and that other people will do what they think is best for them. We can freely choose how we will participate in the reality that is our environment.

Today, I will take every chance to participate in life, not control it.

Be what you are.

When we accept ourselves for what we are — strengths, weaknesses, size, shape — we are on the way to recovery. Many of us didn't like what we were, so we ate to feel better or we dieted to look different, or we did both.

Recovery gets us out of the trap of judging ourselves and others according to external appearances. Recovery teaches us that what's in our minds, hearts, and spirits is more important than how we look, or how we think we look, or how we think others think we look.

We are learning to focus on internals instead of externals — on how we feel, on qualities such as honesty, concern for others, willingness, courage, perseverance. We are learning who we are in relation to other people, what we like to do, what makes us comfortable, how we can be useful, how our gifts and talents can be expressed and shared.

How can I come closer today to being what I am?

Admitting that we don't know puts
us on the path to wisdom.

Our journey toward recovery begins with the admission that we're in trouble, that our answers aren't working, that we need to ask new questions. This open, humble state of mind allows us to learn.

The Twelve Steps describe a learning process that enlightens our feelings and actions as well as our thoughts. We arrive at answers that make a positive difference.

If we brush aside the suggestions of the program, if we dismiss them out of hand because we don't want to try them, we close the door to a method of recovery that has worked for many people. Whether we want to learn to fly an airplane, speak a foreign language, or maintain the process of recovering from an eating disorder, it makes sense to follow the instructions of people who have acquired the necessary skills.

An open mind is one of our most valuable assets. With it, we can find our way out of the maze of counterproductive habits into proven methods of wise living.

What I don't know today can lead me to wisdom.

We define ourselves through our relationships.

What we reveal to our friends helps us to understand ourselves. Inner thoughts and feelings, when shared, become more real and concrete than when we keep them locked inside. How we act with someone else plays a significant role in the development of our character.

Our friends are our teachers — so are family members and colleagues at work. When we believe that the people whose lives touch ours are on our path for a reason, we realize the importance of our contacts with them.

What we learn about ourselves in solitude we can share with those we care about. Through each encounter we learn something more, since another person's perspective expands our self-knowledge. When we open ourselves to another person, we both grow. As we interact with those around us, we help each other grow toward our potential.

Each person I encounter today can show me a piece of myself.

*A friend is someone who supports
our recovery.*

We don't need friends who encourage us,
overtly or subtly, to binge, purge, or restrict. We
don't need friends who fuel our preoccupation
with calories and diets. Sometimes recovery
means making changes in our circle of friends.

The program suggests that we "stick with the
winners," those people who demonstrate that the
Steps are working in their lives. These are the
friends we wish to emulate. We can *catch* recovery from them.

Friends outside the program may also support
our recovery. Understanding and encouragement
may be offered by family members as well. It is
possible, though, that we will be disappointed in
the way some of the people close to us respond to
our efforts to get better. Our recovery may
threaten the status quo of a relationship. When
this happens, it may mean that our commitment
to recovery will require us to make changes in our
circle of friends.

---

*Today, I will seek the winners who are living the
program and who will support my recovery.*

Everything is now.

Recovery teaches us to operate in the present. All we have is today, this moment, and when we delve deeply into now, we find it contains everything we need.

Those of us with an eating disorder tend to put off living until the scales register an "ideal" number of pounds. If we are compulsively perfectionistic about how we look, that day may never arrive. Recovering means accepting ourselves today just as we are today so we can get on with the business of living.

When we concentrate on now, we don't have to be sorry about what we didn't have yesterday or what we might not have tomorrow. We can be what we are today, even if we're not perfect. We can share today's gifts and enjoy them, believing that living well in the present is our best preparation for the future.

I will fully experience the gifts of now.

Do we see the cup as half empty or half full?

If we expect our cup to be always filled to the brim, we may think we never have enough. If we focus on what's lacking in our lives, we will feel deprived. If we look at what we have, we will experience satisfaction, even if everything is not positive.

We choose how we will live — whether we will dwell on the negative or savor the positive, bemoan what we don't have or rejoice in what we do have.

Insisting that our cup should always be full may have played a role in the development of our problems with food. With recovery comes a more balanced perspective. We are learning to avoid the trap of all-or-nothing thinking. We are discovering that it is possible to be satisfied with the good things we have, even if some things still seem to be missing. The more clearly we see how much we already have, the more contented we feel.

Today, I will take a long look at the good things in my life.

*With abstinence, we feel both joy
and sorrow more acutely.*

We can dull our feelings by overeating and numb them by undereating. Both are ways in which we anesthetize our emotions.

Most of us would probably rather not feel pain, but the price of shutting down our feelings is high, since we miss having delightful feelings as well as unpleasant ones. Many of us were so accustomed to concealing our emotions that we weren't sure what it was we were feeling or if we were feeling anything at all!

Once we are eating normally, we begin to experience more deeply how it feels to be angry or sad or afraid. We develop a greater capacity to feel joy and happiness. We find we can ride out emotional ups and downs and learn from them. It is as though we are waking up to a full range of emotions, which are ours to feel and express.

Today, I will not hide from my emotions — they are part of me.

*We can practice forgiveness each
day.*

Resentments have a way of creeping back into
my psyche even after I have let go of them. I know
that holding a grudge is harmful to my emotional
health and can threaten my abstinence, but what
can I do when I keep feeling anger toward
someone?

In the interest of recovery, in my own best interest, I can continue to forgive each day. I may
not be able to forgive the person once and for all,
but I can do it right now, just for today. With practice, who knows? Perhaps the resentment will disappear.

When I remember that my own track record is
far from perfect, I realize I could use some daily
forgiveness too, both from others and from
myself.

---

*Just for now, I can let go of resentments and for-
give. If resentments come back, I can forgive
again.*

Action carries us in the direction we choose.

Recovery involves doing — going to meetings, working our program, reaching out to others. We don't get a job by sitting at home thinking about it, and we don't get a degree by looking at college catalogs.

It's true that we need to reflect; we need quiet times when we pray for guidance. There comes a point, however, when action is called for, when we use the power we are given to carry out our Higher Power's will for our lives to the best of our understanding.

By our actions, we forge new patterns of behavior. We put into practice the wisdom of the Twelve Steps. Your action today can be something as simple as walking out of the kitchen when it's not the right place for you to be, or something as complex as embarking on a training program that will prepare you for a new career.

One action leads to another. Doing what we need to do to be abstinent today adds twenty-four hours to recovery.

Today, I will act on my best understanding of my Higher Power's will for me.

Recovery releases our creativity.

Creativity implies something new — feeling, thinking, acting in a new way. When we step out of a familiar pattern, we often feel anxious. We wonder if the new way will work or if a new venture will succeed. We take a chance, a risk, and that requires courage.

If we refuse to tolerate a certain amount of anxiety, we will stay in our same old ruts. Safe? Perhaps, but stagnant. And maybe not so safe after all, since the opposite of growth is death.

You and I can live creatively if we are willing to have butterflies in our stomachs from time to time. Recovery releases us from old patterns so that we can try new ways of responding to the opportunities we are given each day. Believing we are supported by a Higher Power gives us the courage to take risks, especially when the outcome promises emotional and spiritual growth.

Today, I will dare to follow a creative inner prompting, even if I feel some anxiety.

We cultivate wisdom when we
accept and embrace reality.

Reality is something we cannot change. We can try to deny it, escape it, alter or destroy it, but reality remains intact. Our eating disorder was, in part, an attempt to deny reality. We tried to alter situations we didn't like by eating more or eating less, but the real problems did not get solved either way.

When we are exhausted from our futile efforts to manipulate it, we can relax and let reality be. We may even discover that the way things really are is better than the way we thought we would like them to be.

When we say yes to our world as it is today — just for today — we free ourselves from the cobwebs of illusion so that we can work on what is actual. There may be no easy solutions to our problems, but facing them as they are is infinitely more productive than denying them. The longer we live in the real world, the better we like it.

I pray for the wisdom to make a loving commitment today to what is.

*Aim to be part of the solution, not
part of the problem.*

Each day, we choose the direction we take. We
can complain and make life difficult for ourselves
and those around us. Or we can take constructive
steps toward solving our own problems and also
toward helping someone else. At the very least,
we can resolve to intend no harm.

Being self-absorbed magnifies our emotional
aches, as well as our physical ones. As we turn our
attention to the useful service we can perform for
other people, health and wholeness prosper.

Those of us who are recovering have a unique
opportunity to help each other. We know the
difference understanding and support can make,
both to the person who gives and to the one who
receives. Generosity of spirit can be one of our
daily goals. Displayed often, it produces abundant fruit.

---

*I will be generous today in my efforts to help
others, seeking to solve problems rather than create them.*

Keep it simple.

The less we need, the more freedom we have. If our lives are cluttered with too many obligations, desires, and distractions, then now is the time to clean house and simplify. Since recovery is our number-one priority, we want to take on activities that contribute to getting well and discard those that do not.

What do you really want to do today? Whom do you need to see? What do you need to have? Why not focus on the essentials and forget the complications? Yes, I know, some complicated situations can't be simplified, but others probably can.

Simplicity is beautiful and effective. If we are willing each day to be what we are and no more, we will be open to and at peace with ourselves and the rest of the world.

I will simplify my life today by concentrating on priorities.

Happiness is becoming who we are.

Recovery presents each of us with the challenge of discovering and becoming who we really are. When we take a step, however faltering, in the direction of self-actualization, the reward is joy.

Happiness and joy come from experiencing our potential for growth on all levels — physical, emotional, intellectual, spiritual. They arise from deep within us as we use our ability to appreciate the beauty of a sunset, have fun with our children, understand a friend, or complete a project. Joy cannot be commanded, but when it comes we know we are fully alive and responding to the challenge of self-discovery.

We are fortunate indeed to have found a program that not only shows us how to arrest our eating disorder, but also gives us a blueprint for realizing our potential.

I will not expect perfection or constant happiness, but with my Higher Power's help I will take one small step today toward becoming who I am.

Doing our best is success.

Since we learn by trial and error, we can consider our failures as steps toward success — at the very least, they teach us what not to do. In addition, in Twelve Step programs, we learn that "there is no such thing as failure — there is only slow success."

As long as we are willing to try to maintain abstinence and work the Steps, we are making progress. We need to remember that our eating disorder did not develop overnight, and that solid recovery takes time. Our recovery doesn't rest on magic; instead, it rests on support from our friends and from our Higher Power.

At any given moment, we can do no more than our best. If we are willing to risk putting these best efforts on the line, we will present ourselves to the world as we are right now. And that's success.

I look back and see that my failures are showing me the way to success. I will accept the best I am able to do right now as success for today.

Don't be afraid to be vulnerable.

We shy away from revealing our insecurities, our feelings of inadequacy, our emotional neediness. We play games in an effort to maintain control. Fearful of being rejected, we don't let the other person get close enough to see us as we really are.

If we will put aside our fears just for today, perhaps we can ask for help instead of pretending we have all the answers. We don't want to hide in excess food, and we don't want to numb our feelings with starvation. That means when we have a problem, we need to take it to someone.

Contrary to what we might think, there is strength in vulnerability. We become open and accessible. Since the other person can then respond to who we really are rather than who we pretend to be, we can build authentic relationships. Being vulnerable goes along with being alive and human.

I will accept my vulnerability today and realize it can bring me closer to others.

Conflict is a part of intimacy.

Being close to another person means we will inevitably clash. If we relate to each other as the separate individuals we are, without suppressing our honest feelings and reactions, conflicts are bound to arise. The question is, how do we handle them?

It is through experiencing conflicts and working them out with those we love that intimacy is deepened. The alternative is to refrain from caring, avoiding conflict with people who are not particularly important to us.

Intimacy opens us to hurt and anger. What divides us must be acknowledged and negotiated if the relationship is to be a growing, vital one. Using the Twelve Steps, we have tools for working through conflicts. As we recover, we learn how to communicate effectively with those we love instead of withdrawing into food abuse.

Is there a conflict I need to face today? I will remember that intimacy is worth fighting for!

*Recovery means understanding my
body's signals.*

My body knows many things of which my mind
is as yet unaware. If I try to make my body go
against its own wisdom in order to obey my mind,
the result may be an internal mutiny or a civil war
or an eating disorder.

As I recover, I learn to feel how much is enough
— enough food, rest, exercise, sex, work, play. I
pay attention to the needs of my body, because if
I don't, my body will rebel.

When I get in touch on a deep level with how
my body is feeling and what it knows — as well
as what my mind thinks and my spirit understands
— insight occurs. Then I am integrated within myself and can act out of a totality of body, mind, and
spirit. Genuine awareness makes the wisdom of
my body available to my conscious mind.

---

*I will be aware of the inner signals my body is
sending me right now. Instead of brushing them
aside, I will be quiet and pay attention to them.*

Security is being able to risk appearing foolish.

As we follow the Steps into a firm relationship with a Higher Power, we become less concerned about being right and looking good to the outside world and more concerned with expressing how we feel. Someone else may think we're wrong, inept, unsophisticated, or foolish, but so what? Our goal is to be authentic, true to ourselves. If we do or say something dumb, as we probably will from time to time, our world will not fall apart.

Few experiences are more joyless than constantly monitoring ourselves in case we make what someone else believes to be a mistake. We become tied up in self-consciousness, and we don't have any fun. Sensing our distress, those around us don't have much fun either.

When we place our security in the hands of a Higher Power, we can relax into the joy of spontaneity. We can laugh at our own foolishness and let others laugh with us.

I will have the courage today to appear foolish. I will take time to have some fun.

April

Even when life doesn't make sense,
we can still maintain abstinence.

Abstinence — eating what we need for good health and not bingeing or starving — makes sense for us even, and especially, when the rest of our world seems crazy and out of control.

Often, it is only when we look back on what has happened that we see that our life pattern has meaning. We may then be able to understand an event which, at the time it occurred, was at best disappointing. Then again, sometimes not even the perspective of time can bring understanding. Sometimes we simply have to trust that a Higher Power is in control of what to us appears incomprehensible.

Whatever happens today, we are best able to deal with it when our bodies are properly nourished and when our attention is fixed on the program goals of emotional and spiritual growth. The longer we maintain abstinence and work the Steps, the better the pieces of our lives seem to fit together.

May I remember today that with abstinence comes order.

Courage grows as we use it.

When we are willing to trust our instincts and follow the promptings of our inner voice, then all we may need is a small amount of courage to reach our goals.

In the past, fear and discouragement may have threatened to overwhelm us. We may have distracted ourselves from our fear by overeating, purging, or restricting. Now we are finding that when we really want to do something — want it for ourselves and not just to please someone else — we are willing to risk failure and go directly after what we want.

Small successes build our confidence. The courage to ask for a raise we deserve can grow into enough courage to change jobs if we feel that is the right move to make. The courage to ask for help with a problem can become the courage to make desirable changes in our lifestyle. The more we draw from our spiritual storehouse, the more bravely we pursue our dreams and aspirations.

I will use my supply of courage today so that I will have more tomorrow.

Life moves forward.

The past is past — over — finished. Our job is to move with the flow of the present. We are propelled by what went before, but we do not try to swim against the current of our present lives by regretting or yearning for old times.

Each day of recovery releases us from the past and gives us a fresh start. We can put behind us the misery of compulsive behavior — we certainly don't yearn to re-experience that! Though the good times of the past will stay in our memories, our minds need to be focused on the present.

Recovery also readies us for the future: We don't fear what lies ahead, since it is in the hands of our Higher Power. Our task is to earnestly seek to know and do our Higher Power's will for us today so that we will keep moving with the stream of goodness that wends through our lives. Trust and confidence support us as we face forward.

Working my program today keeps me steady in the present and ready for the future.

*When we feel out of sorts, we can
resolve to at least do ourselves no
harm.*

There are some days when we feel as though we
are standing still, making no progress whatsoever.
We may feel depressed, sluggish, bored, or generally lacking the motivation to do the things we
had planned to do.

These are the days when we can profit from extra attention to our program — some additional
reading, perhaps, or more phone calls. They are
also times when we can say, "Okay, I may not
make visible progress today. I may not be in a very
good mood. But at the very least, I can avoid self-
destructive behavior around food. I can follow
my food plan for today, whether or not I feel like
it."

If we don't fuel a bad mood by overeating or
undereating, we have a better chance of getting
over it quickly. One of the best ways to escape
boredom and depression is by getting involved in
something outside ourselves — for instance, doing something for someone else.

*If today promises to be "one of those days," I will
do some extra work on my program.*

We can disagree with those we love.

In our efforts to please other people, those of us with eating disorders sometimes stifle our own valid opinions, going along with another person's ideas at the expense of our own. This leaves us wide open to the kind of inner resentment that does the relationship no good, erodes our self-esteem, and feeds our eating disorder.

Our opinions are worthwhile and deserve to be heard. With recovery comes increased self-confidence; we are able to be effectively assertive about issues important to us. We learn how to disagree constructively instead of flying into a rage or quietly seething.

Dialogue is at the heart of our relationships with those we love. Genuine dialogue means an open exchange where each of us has a chance to listen and be heard. By exploring our differences, we keep the relationship alive and growing. By working through our conflicts, we arrive at a deeper understanding of each other.

I will express a valid, honest opinion today, even if it means disagreeing with someone close to me.

*In the long run, it's easier to carry
out our Higher Power's will than
our own.*

The good news of the Twelve Step program is that we don't have to continue trying to make self-will work. Attempting to make the rest of the world conform to what we think we want is a little like trying to push water uphill. It's not only frustrating — it's exhausting.

Getting in touch with a Higher Power frees us from the trap of self-will. We can move with the rhythm of reality instead of being stuck in fantasy. We can discover how we can be useful and what it is we do best.

How can I be sure I'm doing my Higher Power's will? There is, of course, no certain way to know, but what I rely on is an inner sense of lightness and rightness. I pray for guidance, I ask for answers, I listen to my inner voice, and I talk to people whose opinion I respect. I also believe if what I'm doing is not my Higher Power's will for me, I'll find out, since it won't work.

I ask to know my Higher Power's will for me today and for the ability to carry it out.

We attract what we project.

If we meet our world, and the people in it, with a smile and the confidence that it's going to be a good day, we're likely to get a positive response. Recovery teaches us that we're responsible for our attitudes. We can decide to seek happiness or to remain unhappy, to be negative or positive. Which do you choose today?

No matter where we are, we take with us our moods, our hopes, our beliefs, our dreams, our habits. We take with us attitudes about ourselves and other people. As we recover, we like ourselves better, and these good feelings are reflected onto and from those around us.

We can cultivate enthusiasm, concern and caring for others, and faith that "God is doing for us what we could not do for ourselves."* The more we focus on developing positive attitudes, the more we find them in other people. It's true — like attracts like.

Today I will try to be what I want to attract.

Alcoholics Anonymous (New York: Alcoholics Anonymous World Services, Inc., 1955), p. 84.

Together we can continue to recover.

Recovery is a never ending process. We can always get better. When we are able to eat reasonably and healthfully and maintain a normal weight, we still continue to work on the emotional and spiritual aspects of recovery, the problems of living from which none of us is exempt.

We need to share our concerns with each other so we do not slip back into isolation and so we can benefit from mutual support. We need to talk to friends who understand, who care about us, and who will give us honest feedback.

Clearly, we could not manage our eating disorder alone, and we need each other to continue the process of getting better. Fortunately, the Twelve Step program provides us with supportive companionship that helps us stay on track, avoid relapse, and make progress in all areas of our lives. We're very lucky to have found answers that work. We can cultivate the humility that acknowledges our need for each other.

I will make contact today with a program friend.

*We can't command serenity, but we
can invite it.*

Recovery does not guarantee perpetual calmness and tranquility. We are still subject to the same stress and pressure that we used to try to handle by eating too much or too little. The difference is that we now have a better way of dealing with it.

As we go through the Steps, we get ourselves off center stage. We spend less time trying to control and direct. We come to believe there is meaning to our lives and a plan that we can follow. We believe that the challenges that come to us arrive for a reason, and that we can learn from them.

When events seem to get out of hand and we feel distraught and upset, we know where to go. We know there is a calm, quiet place in the center of ourselves where serenity lies waiting. We can't force serenity to appear, but we can consciously let go of our stress and tension and wait for the peace the program promises us.

I invite serenity today by centering myself in quiet meditation.

A friend is someone who accepts us as we are.

The way we get better is by first accepting who we are and where we are right now. If you are my friend, you affirm me as I am today. This increases my confidence and courage so that I am free to change and be better tomorrow.

In recovery, when our attention is no longer fixed on food, we can expand our circle of caring and find the genuine, nurturing kind of friendship we need. As we grow in self-esteem, we become willing to disclose more of who we really are to our special friends.

If I trust you as my friend, I can risk being candid and vulnerable. By sharing my hopes and dreams, my fears and feelings of inadequacy, I learn more about myself. I feel known and accepted, and I am encouraged to become the best that I can be.

How wonderful it is to find people who care and understand! We will find them — as we follow our path, as we risk being open and candid, and as we offer to others the same acceptance we want to receive.

On my path today, I will be ready to give and receive real friendship.

We come to know our friends by letting them know us.

Eating disorders push us into isolation. More and more, we withdraw from those close to us, in the mistaken assumption that bingeing and dieting will give us what we need. They don't, of course.

We get to know another person by becoming willing to disclose who we are. Then our friend can also risk disclosure. If we only skim the surface of our relationship, neither of us receives the emotional nurturing we need.

Friendship is an exchange of thoughts, feelings, and actions. The more genuinely we each give of ourselves, the more we receive. We are mutually nourished.

Those of us who are recovering with the help of a Higher Power and the Twelve Steps can become more open and candid with the people who are important to us. In so doing, we deepen our friendships and escape the isolation that was part of our illness.

When there is an opportunity to disclose myself to a friend today, I will take it.

With love, our world falls into place.

We are searchers. We look for what will satisfy our deepest longings, and we sometimes look in strange places. We look in the refrigerator, in the bottom of a glass, at a sports car or designer clothes — and we are disappointed.

But we keep searching, and if we're persistent, we move beyond material things (which are good, but in themselves, not enough) into the realm of the heart and spirit. There we learn about the kind of love that engages our total personality.

We love with body, heart, mind, and spirit. We become integrated, and so does our perception of the world around us.

Love is what makes us feel whole and complete. If we are to receive it, we have to give it. In order to continue improving our ability to give love, we continue the journey of recovery.

The more complete my recovery, the more love I will be able to give, and the more love I give, the more love I receive.

*Recovery brings us the ability to
choose.*

Compulsive patterns — when we're not trapped in them, putting forth the same old destructive responses to the same old problems, we learn to make positive choices. One positive choice leads to another, and before long we suddenly realize that life is really getting better.

People — we can choose those with whom we will spend our time. We can choose friends who give us support, who help us with our program of recovery. We can avoid spending time with people who threaten our progress. Sometimes this means making changes that are difficult initially but that contribute to developing long-term serenity. We have a choice.

Places and activities — we can put ourselves in places where we are comfortable, and we can do things that bring us joy and satisfaction. Sometimes we need to say no to places that might cause us to slip and to activities that frustrate us. We have the ability to choose.

Our Higher Power is on the side of positive choices.

I will realize how many positive choices are available to me today.

The further we progress in recovery,
the greater our capacity for intimacy.

Our eating disorder was a sidetrack diverting our attention from the main track of living. Now that we're back on the main track, we're more aware of the need for intimacy and better able to meet that need. We know recovery depends on our willingness to nurture close relationships with people important to us.

We start where we are. We work on strengthening and deepening the friendships we already have, and we open ourselves to opportunities to meet new people and develop new ties. The Twelve Step program is a natural source of contacts for expanding our circle of friends and getting to know other people in satisfying and significant ways. So is our family and place of work.

Do we really know our friends and those with whom we live and work? The more we are willing to be honest and risk disclosure, the more liberated we will be from addictive patterns of thought and action. The more we can genuinely care about the other person, the greater our capacity for satisfying and creative intimacy.

May today's abstinence lead me into ever-deepening intimacy.

Our bodies are probably wiser than we think.

Each of us has an ideal weight range, determined by our height, age, and body type. Each of us has the capacity to know how it feels to have eaten the right amount of food, to be satisfied with what our bodies need. Each of us also has a bodily awareness of what else we need — rest, exercise, warmth, love, stimulation.

Ideally, the mind and the body function together as a whole. When they don't, we're in trouble. By respecting the wisdom of the body, we can avoid being driven by mental compulsions that lead us to abuse our bodies, minds, and spirits through restricting or bingeing.

How do we do this? Those of us who have problems with food can become more aware of the messages we get from our bodies. We can explore our feelings of hunger, or our aversion to eating, until we reach the emotional issues that underlie them. Our eating disorder is a symptom. The body is telling us something. What is yours telling you?

I will listen today to the messages my body sends me. I will seek to understand its wisdom.

I can treat myself well, whatever the scale reports.

How thin is thin enough? What do I have to weigh in order to be acceptable?

These are questions we ask when we realize we may be endangering our physical and emotional health in the attempt to conform to what we think is ideal. Our society extols slenderness, and some of us have made it our number-one goal.

Yes, we want to be fit and attractive, but we are discovering there is much more to life than external appearance and numbers on a scale. As we learn to eat for health, we put aside obsession with weight and allow ourselves to develop new interests.

Our program directs our attention away from weight toward the building of a rich emotional and spiritual life. Once we commit ourselves to an appropriate food plan, we can let our body make its own adjustments gradually while we get on with the rest of life. We can be kind and patient with ourselves in our progress toward recovery.

I will be good to myself today and let my food plan take care of my weight.

Silence heals.

Noise is all around us. We are bombarded with sounds of traffic, voices, music, machines — even our own thoughts are often noisy. We can become so accustomed to noise that we are uncomfortable when there aren't any sounds to distract us. Making noise is a way of escaping from what we fear would be the boredom, emptiness, and silence of our inner selves.

Sometimes what we fear is exactly what we need! How restful and restorative it is to sink into the silence of an empty space when we are tired and jangled. How peaceful to be able to let go of agitating thoughts. How healing to turn off the machines and close our mouths for a period of quiet.

When I'm hurting, I don't need extra food, but I do need extra peace and quiet. By being silent I can get in touch with my inner strength. For me, silence is a powerful tool of recovery.

Today, I will take time to be still and experience the healing power of silence.

*If abstinence is boring, then our
thoughts and our lives may still be
centered on food.*

Those of us who were bingers used food for fun
and excitement, to some degree. In part, those of
us who restricted ourselves found excitement in
severely limiting what we ate. Now that we are abstinent, we may wonder how to fill up our time
and where to direct our attention.

The beauty of abstinence is that we can decide
on a reasonable, healthy meal plan and then let go
of the obsession with food and diets. We are free
to find absorbing, enjoyable things to do, things
that help us grow emotionally and spiritually. We
can try new activities, meet new people, get out
of our old ruts.

Abstinence opens new doors. We discover that
it was bingeing and restricting that were boring,
because they limited our other options. Abstinent, we are wide open to new possibilities.

*May I seek excitement that enhances my recovery
today.*

Sometimes we need to be empty.

Sometimes it's good to be quiet and alone. How else do we become acquainted with the inner self? If we're constantly bombarded by external stimuli — noise, people, activities, demands — we risk losing our center, or never finding it.

Our impulse often is to try to fill ourselves up — with food, possessions, thoughts, plans, worries, accomplishments. We fear being empty, as though if we were empty we might very well cease to exist. We fear the void within.

Meditation teaches us that being empty is not a dreadful experience. On the contrary, when we empty ourselves of our busyness, we are refreshed and recreated. We are able to receive insights and hear what our deeper self has to tell us. Spending some time each day being quiet and alone puts us in touch with our center and enables us to listen to the inner voice.

I will take at least five minutes today to be alone and quiet.

Is there room in your day for the unexpected?

Recovery works best for me when I'm open to what comes along each day. I used to set rigid schedules for myself, write long lists of things to do, and proceed through the day wearing the blinders of my preconceived scenario. Binges were my way of rebelling against my own rigidity and also a protest against whatever upset my carefully made plans.

We miss a lot when we try to impose our own structure on the events of the day. Perhaps we do it out of anxiety, and perhaps we do it to feel we're in control, but it doesn't work.

However hard we try to ignore or prevent the unexpected, the unexpected occurs. One of the things recovery teaches us is that we can trust ourselves and our Higher Power to deal with whatever comes along. Whether good or not-so-good, no event requires us to binge or restrict. Instead, using our inner resources, we are free to respond spontaneously to the real-life situations that we encounter.

Today, I will be open to the unexpected. Who knows? It might be fun!

Without a crutch, everything is real.

It's an exciting experience to live each day without dulling our senses with the anesthetic of excess food, bingeing and perhaps purging, or self-starvation. Without these familiar props, however, we may have considerable anxiety. There is no longer a buffer to deaden our feelings.

What we do have are tools for managing the anxiety, tools that build us up rather than tear us down. We have friends in the program with whom we can share our fears and who help us put our anxieties in perspective. We practice Steps that nurture a healthy dependence on a Power greater than ourselves. And we have the growing confidence that with abstinence, all things are possible. We can become strong enough to face our anxieties and function in spite of them.

To some of us, it may seem as though we're going back emotionally to the age when our eating disorder began, and that we're relearning how to manage the problems we used to cover up with food or diets. Scary, perhaps, but how exciting to be living in the real world!

Today, I am thankful for not to be using over- or undereating as a crutch.

What underlies my problem with food?

Those of us who have eating disorders have translated our major problems into a language of food, diets, weight, and calories. When we thought in this language and were controlled by it, we lost sight of our real problems.

If I am never satisfied, no matter how much I eat or how little I weigh, then my problem is not food or weight — it is low self-esteem. Discovering why my self-esteem is low and how I can improve it contributes to my recovery, since the reasons for my low self-esteem undergird my problem with food.

Once we accept abstinence — eating the food we need and not bingeing, purging, or restricting — our food problem is taken care of. Now we are free to focus our attention on making positive changes in our attitudes, actions, and lifestyle.

Underneath our surface food problem are issues of relationships, self-esteem, communication, vocation and career, identity — the list goes on. With dedicated effort and the guidance of a Higher Power, we will find solutions.

Today, I will be aware of the problems I encounter in living.

Sensuality belongs to our recovering self.

An important part of recovery is integrating our sensual self with our spiritual self. Our bodies are to be loved and enjoyed. If we neglect or denigrate our sensuality, we shut ourselves off from the pleasurable feelings that are our birthright as physical beings. So a prime task of recovery is to come to terms with the interrelationship between the physical and the spiritual, between body and soul.

As a guideline, "I'll do anything as long as it feels good" defeats its own purpose if it results in excess, which soon does not feel good at all. The goal of sensual pleasure by itself is not sufficient if by pursuing it we ignore our emotional and spiritual needs.

How do we become integrated? Interestingly enough, spiritual growth can enhance the appreciation and enjoyment of our sensuality. Self-respect translates into taking good care of our body, accepting it, loving it, living in it, and giving ourselves permission to enjoy it.

Today, I will accept and nurture both my body and spirit.

Whether the parenting we received
was good, bad, or indifferent, the
responsibility for our lives is now
ours.

As we unravel the tangled skeins of our obsession with food and diets, we may be tempted to look for a convenient hook on which to hang the problem. Parents often seem to be the most readily available receptacles of blame for whatever malfunctioning we exhibit. When it comes to eating disorders, mothers are particularly vulnerable to complaints.

Since none of us exists in a vacuum, it's true that our family system plays a crucial role in the attitudes and behavior we develop. Examining our feelings about food and our individual eating patterns, we can begin to identify and understand how they have been influenced by the kind of parenting we had.

Understanding is the first step toward loosening the cords and laying to rest old conflicts and hurts. Blaming and complaining are not routes toward recovery. Forgiveness and tolerance are. As adults, we become responsible for ourselves and for our own parenting.

Today, I will be my own best parent.

Setting limits fosters recovery.

The boundary lines we draw for ourselves delineate a safe area within which our recovery can flourish. We set limits with regard to food — what, when, and how much — so that we can maintain good health. We also set limits on what we do and say, how we spend our time and money, whom we choose to be our friends.

Setting limits makes life more satisfying. Much of our stress results from being unclear about our boundaries: what we need as opposed to what we want, what is necessary for us to do and what is optional, what is life-enhancing and what goes against health and integrity. Knowing when to stop and when to say no reduces frustration and saves us from making emotionally costly mistakes.

We said no to the incapacitating effects of an eating disorder when we accepted abstinence and the principles of the Twelve Step program. Organizing our lives this way reduces stress, since we have solid support to rely on and a simple maxim to remember: when in doubt, don't.

I will move toward recovery today by setting limits.

*An ounce of compassion is worth a
pound of advice.*

When people tell us what to do, our resistance
rises. "If I were you," begins a friend. "But you're
not me," we protest silently or aloud. Instead of
someone who will tell us what to do, we want
someone who will listen to us, feel with us, understand us, and validate our struggles and our tenta-
tive solutions.

We know this, and yet how quickly we ourselves become advice-givers. You come to me
with a problem, and I think I have to fix it. I am
uncomfortable with your pain and distress, and
so I want to brush it away. I am uncomfortable
with my own sense of inadequacy if I can't come
up with a ready response.

Compassion heals distress and smooths our
way toward finding our own answers. Rather
than advice, the Twelve Steps offer suggestions
based on experience. Following the Steps into a
deepening spiritual awareness, we develop
greater compassion for all whom we encounter,
including ourselves.

*I will open my heart today to the healing power
of compassion.*

We can't solve other people's problems, but we can listen.

I can't tell you what to do, but I can listen to you and respond with honesty and sensitivity to what you say. By sharing your concerns with me, you will understand them more clearly, put them in perspective, and be able to see possibilities for constructive action.

Giving up our attempts to control other people's lives is part of the recovery process. We come to believe that those close to us are being guided by a Higher Power just as we are, that they will find their own solutions, and that they will grow and develop at their own pace.

What we can give to those we love is our attention and care. We can be available to them physically, emotionally, and spiritually with the kind of undemanding, nonjudging support that helps them find their way. When we stop trying to control, our listening creates a climate conducive to growth.

When someone needs me to listen today, I will give them my full attention.

• APRIL 28 •

Recovery requires action.

It seems like it would be a great gift if someone could wave a magic wand over us and produce instant recovery, but that's not the way it works. To recover from our eating disorder, we need to actively change our behavior.

We have tried to use food and diets to fill needs that neither can fill. Recovery involves identifying these needs and finding effective ways of meeting them. If we have withdrawn from other people, we can take action to form relationships that will nurture us emotionally. We can reach out for the kind of support that our lives have lacked.

Going to OA meetings, making food plans, using the telephone, finding interesting work to do, helping other people, having fun — all of these are actions that build recovery. We can't sit back and expect to get well magically. What we can do is take the next action that will move us in the right direction, the direction in which our Higher Power is prompting us to go.

What action toward recovery will I take today?

We find our center in solitude.

Solitude is not something to escape. We can learn how to be alone comfortably and creatively. There is no better way to find out who we are and how we can open ourselves to a relationship with a Higher Power than by spending time alone regularly.

Fear of being alone sends us looking for distractions, and sometimes the distractions we find are unhealthy. Part of our fear of solitude comes from not wanting to encounter our darker side. We try to cover up this fear with too much or too little food, with chemicals, and with unsatisfying relationships, which we grasp onto as a way of avoiding our inner selves.

It is in solitude that we hear most clearly our inner voice. The insights we receive help us define who we are and where we are going. Centering ourselves in meditation gives us a spiritual base for the day, one to which we may return whenever serenity is threatened. Recovery teaches us that solitude is not to be feared or avoided but used and enjoyed, and that every part of us is acceptable.

I will not be afraid to spend some time alone today.

*Playing "catch up" requires time
and patience.*

Many of us developed an eating disorder in childhood or adolescence. We tried to make food or compulsive dieting fill our emotional needs, and this prevented us from growing up at the pace and time we should have. As a result, some of us feel that our emotional development was arrested when our eating disorder began, and that only with recovery are we beginning to "catch up" to our chronological age.

That's okay. We can only begin where we are, and we need to be patient with ourselves. Because we used food to dull our childhood and adolescent pain and insecurity, we can expect some of those unpleasant feelings to surface during recovery. The difference is that now we have help for dealing with them.

We don't have to continue responding to life in the same old way. We can change. We can grow. If we will invest the necessary time and patience, playing "catch up" can be an exciting adventure.

Today, I will be patient with myself and take the time I need to grow up emotionally.

May

Food is not for revenge.

For most of us, self-stravation was an attempt to hurt and control those who love us. It may have been a reaction to an overcontrolling parent, someone who felt she or he knew what was best for us and who brooked no opposition. Bingeing may also have been a form of revenge: "You hurt me, so I'll show you!"

But what happened? We were the ones who suffered ill health, not whomever we thought we were punishing. The revenge backfired, and we ourselves became the primary target. Someone else may have suffered too, distressed for us, but our own body received the brunt of the punishment.

A better plan is to turn over our desire for revenge to a Higher Power and concentrate on getting the most we can out of life, one day at a time. Food is for nourishing our bodies, not for getting even with someone else or for compensating for a feeling of having been shortchanged.

Getting even is not on my agenda today.

What counts is doing the best we can with what we have.

Most of us would like to be more — more attractive, more talented, more successful, more popular, more competent. Many of us may have been overachievers, trying to compensate for what we felt we lacked and focusing much of our discontent on food and our bodies. Most of us would also probably like to have more — more time, more money, more approval, more love.

Our program of recovery guides us into a deeper appreciation of the gifts and blessings we have right now. When we tune in to the present, we are able to tap the resources we already possess. We don't need to wait until our bodies acquire an ideal shape to enjoy them. We don't have to move to a bigger house to make friends. And we don't need to win awards to make a useful contribution with what we have where we are.

Right now, we can love the people who are in our lives, without waiting until we become better or they become more deserving. We may not win prizes or beauty contests, but we can have the satisfaction of using our gifts and talents responsibly, as recovery makes them available to us.

Today, I will use what I have with gratitude.

*Giving love unconditionally — this
is the way to live.*

When we are in touch with our inner self and
our Higher Power, we are able to love others
without attaching strings and conditions. How
wonderfully free we are when we can give love to
someone else without exacting or expecting a
return! We don't have to worry about whether
the recipient deserves our love or returns it — we
can just give it, and in so doing feel whole and full.

Unconditional love heals. It heals us personally,
and it heals relationships. Even if the other person
rejects our love, we have gained strength and
peace through being able to give it. And the door
is open for a future deepening of the relationship.

When we love unconditionally, we are reflecting the love that comes to us from a Higher Power.
It is always available as long as we are willing to let
it flow through us to those with whom we come
in contact. We don't have to wait for them to love
us first or to fulfill our expectations. We can accept them just as they are, because we are sharing
the unconditional love we receive.

*The love I give today makes me feel whole and
happy.*

*The first step toward correcting a
mistake is admitting we made one.*

We all make mistakes, and when we do, we
have a method for dealing with them. Step Ten of
our program suggests taking a daily inventory and
promptly admitting when we are wrong. If I have
indeed made a mistake, stubbornly trying to cling
to and defend my position is counterproductive.
When I acknowledge that I have been wrong, the
door to correcting the mistake swings open.

We can realize we won't always be right. We
can work on developing enough humility so that
we recognize our part in a misunderstanding. We
can be willing to reevaluate our decisions and
actions.

When I admit I made a mistake, I drop my
defenses. This enables and encourages you to
drop your defenses also, and the two of us are better able to reach an understanding. When we are
genuinely interested in following the best course
of action, we can both move beyond the mistake
and correct the problem.

May I not be too proud to admit my mistakes.

Getting to know a Higher Power means we don't have to expect the worst.

I used to think that if I worried enough about something, maybe it wouldn't happen. Most of the things I worried about didn't happen, but some not-so-good things that I didn't worry about did happen.

So far I haven't found a way of completely avoiding unpleasant occurrences. What I have found, though, is that by living the Twelve Steps to the best of my ability, I can worry less about what doesn't happen and cope better with what does.

One day at a time, I believe I get what I need. Today may not go exactly according to my fantasies, but neither is it likely to approach my worst imaginings. Since I found the Steps, most days have been much better than my expectations. I can now take things as they come, trusting that I will receive the resources I need.

Today, I will remember that worry creates a barrier between me and my Higher Power.

*We sculpt our lives by getting rid of
what doesn't belong.*

Someone once described the work of a sculptor
as that of chiseling away all of the stone that isn't
a part of the work of art. So, too, we discover who
we are by eliminating what gets in the way and
hampers our development. We say no to what we
don't want to be and do, in order to more fully
realize our true potential.

We become abstinent and eat what we need for
optimum health. Slowly, our bodies emerge from
being overfed or undernourished, taking on the
shape that is best for us. This is just the beginning.
Along with being selective about what we eat, we
also become selective about what we do, how we
think, how we interact with other people. We become aware of the negative characteristics that
got in our way, and we turn them over to a Higher
Power.

The Twelve Step program teaches us to simplify our lives. We feel good, new energy becomes available to us, and we learn how to choose
the people and activities that nurture our recovery. Daily, our true values emerge.

*I ask my Higher Power to teach me to accept
myself.*

*If abstinence falls apart, we can
begin again.*

Slips and slides do happen, but all is not lost.
Once we experience how good we feel when we
are eating what our bodies need, we will not be
happy when we slip away from our food plan.

We do not have to stay away for long. No matter
what time of day the slip occurs, we can get right
back on track. Often we need outside help, which
may mean talking to a friend or sponsor about
what's bothering us. It may mean reading program literature. Maybe what we need is to sit
quietly for a few moments and get in touch with
a source of strength and power greater than
our own.

Slips and slides should not become excuses for
giving up. Thoughts of "I didn't do it perfectly, so
I might as well blow the whole thing" can be ex-
changed for a reassuring idea: "Okay, so I slipped
— now the slip is over, and at this moment I'm abstinent again." Sometimes we need to begin again
several times a day. That's okay. We're learning.

---

*Today, I give myself permission to begin again
with whatever I am trying to learn.*

Discovering who I am is a continual adventure.

When compulsion rules, we aren't sure who we are, since the obsession with food and diets threatens to take over our personality. We don't have much time or energy left for self-discovery.

Putting food in its proper place—eating moderate meals that nourish our bodies—allows us the freedom to find out what we like to do, make friends who share our interests, develop a career, and enrich our emotional and spiritual lives. We come out of our self-imposed isolation and discover that other people are there for us when we are willing to be open, candid, and caring.

We discover ourselves in relation to the activities we enjoy, to the people with whom we come in contact, and to a Higher Power. We need these outside sources of stimulation and support — food and diets are not enough.

Discovery often involves risk, as we leave the security of the known and familiar in order to grow. We try something new, and if it doesn't work, we try something else. Life becomes an adventure.

May I courageously continue the adventure of self-discovery.

*Recovery gives us back to those we
love.*

When we were bingeing, purging, starving, or
obsessed with food and diets, we were not as
emotionally available to the important people in
our lives as we would like to have been. Addictive
behavior takes us out of circulation and away
from meaningful contacts.

We may have blamed those close to us for our
problems with food or stopped communicating
because we felt they didn't understand. The inventory and amends Steps suggest we take
responsibility for our behavior and consider
specific ways of repairing the interpersonal damage that occurred. We have a chance to rebuild
relationships on firmer ground, with new sensitivity and greater awareness of how our words
and actions affect those we love.

Recovery teaches us to be receptive to the signals we are given, rather than avoiding or escaping them. Dialogue becomes possible. We listen
and are present, participating in the challenge of
actively relating to others.

*I will be available today to the significant people
in my life.*

Abstinence unlocks our potential.

Recovering from an eating disorder means relearning how to eat moderate meals and how to abstain from bingeing or starving. When abstinence is firmly established, we are free to become the people we are meant to be. No longer obsessed and preoccupied with food and diets, we can use the released energy to develop our potential.

How do I know what I am capable of doing until I try? Perhaps I was afraid to try in the past, and perhaps that was a reason I was preoccupied with food and diets. With abstinence, I am free to go back to where I stopped developing my talents and abilities and to see what I can do with them.

I will remember today that my recovery is only as good as my abstinence, and that in order to make progress in the areas of love and work, I need to follow my food plan. I am grateful to have found a way out of my eating disorder into a fuller life.

My first priority today is the moderate, healthy eating that will allow me to develop my potential.

*Our Higher Power doesn't expect
more than we can deliver.*

There are times when all of us experience feelings of inadequacy, when we are filled with doubt
and wonder how we will ever meet the challenges
we face. Some of us have spent too much time
feeling we are not good enough, that we will
never live up to our expectations and those of
others.

Our recovery program offers a way to get rid of
these feelings of inadequacy. We take the Steps,
especially Step Eleven — seeking knowledge of a
Higher Power's will for us and strength to carry it
out. This means we are now concerned with
measuring up to our Higher Power's expectations, and that all the help we need is constantly
available to us.

It is reassuring to believe there is a plan for our
lives that coordinates with the strengths and abilities we possess. We're only required to be and do
what fits our capabilities. Each day is an invitation
to turn to our Higher Power and to continue to
discover what those capabilities are.

*I believe whatever my Higher Power expects of me
today is within my capacity.*

*I am responsible for my own feel-
ings and actions.*

In recovery, we learn to feel the feelings we formerly anesthetized with food or starved away.
We become willing to experience them and take
responsibility for them. We learn, too, that our actions are our own responsibility. We choose to do
what we do.

Blaming other people for how we felt or what
we did left us feeling helpless. Those other people
appeared to be controlling our lives. No longer
are we caught in that trap. We can choose our
responses.

You may do or say something that hurts me. I
can feel the hurt, and then I can choose how to respond. I may feel anger, but I can choose what I
will do with the anger. I am learning how to acknowledge my feelings without acting in ways
that injure my body or poison my emotional state.
I am responsible for my health and well-being.
What you do and say will affect me, of course, but
I am responsible for how I react.

Today, I can choose how I will act on my feelings.

*We don't need to cling to something
that is not ours to have.*

The ability to let go will save us countless hours of frustration and emotional wear and tear. Now that we have turned our food and weight problem over to a Higher Power, we can also turn over our other problems.

We can let go of a relationship if it is not in our best interest or if the other person has let go of us. In the same way, we can let go of the outcome of a job search, an important project, the sale of a house. None of this is easy to do. We'd prefer to be in control, to determine the results according to what we think we want.

Experience helps us believe that if we are supposed to have something, we will have it. If not, if one door closes, we have seen many times that another door opens. Clinging to what is not really ours is an exercise in futility. How much more pleasant it is to accept today's gifts and let go of the rest!

I believe that today life will give me what I am supposed to have.

As we think, so we become.

We can enrich our interior monologue. We can seek the company of people who inspire us with a loving approach to life. We can absorb the written thoughts of writers who encourage our positive emotions. We can decide to be cheerful and optimistic, just for today.

Whom would you rather be around — someone who chronically complains and talks about what a mess everything is, or someone who finds joy and delight in watching the antics of two squirrels in a tree? You are your constant companion. Your own company can be a pleasure or a drag, depending on the thoughts and feelings you permit to linger in your consciousness.

We take Steps Four and Five in order to sort out our thoughts, getting rid of those that depress our spirit. In Step Ten, we continue a daily mental housecleaning so that residues of resentment and discouragement are not allowed to accumulate. Then we go on to Step Eleven for an infusion of the kind of thinking that nurtures the person we want to become.

Today, I will exercise my freedom of thought.

Tired? Time for a change.

Some of us treated fatigue with food. Others of us found that feelings of boredom and depression sent us in the opposite direction, away from food.

Neither eating too much nor eating too little is the antidote to feeling tired. Maybe all we need is physical rest, a good night's sleep. But if the fatigue persists, or if we've already had enough rest, perhaps we need to introduce some change into our lives.

Often, we feel tired when faced with something we don't want to do. We resist whatever it is; something inside of us is saying no. Instead of resorting to too much or too little food, we can analyze the source of our fatigue and make positive changes.

Perhaps the problem is a job that is no longer challenging or fulfilling. Perhaps we need to make new friends, find new hobbies or activities, eliminate unnecessary drains on time and energy. Perhaps the remedy is as simple as a short walk.

Today, I ask for the courage to change the things I can.

We can create an inner refuge.

Pressures build, tension attacks, and we need to find ways to relax. We get tired, confusion seems endless, and we yearn to anchor ourselves in a quiet, peaceful place.

Picture yourself in a calm harbor. The gentle waves lap against your boat, lulling you with a soft, rocking motion. Everything is quiet. You have all the time you need to sink into tranquility. Each of your needs is taken care of. You take deep breaths. You are at peace.

The first few times you visit your inner harbor, you may feel some anxiety and restlessness. Practice letting go of them. The more often you spend time in this inner refuge, the more comfortable and peaceful you will become.

We can carve out a quiet place in the center of ourselves where we can return frequently for rest and relaxation. We can create an inner refuge where we will be refreshed and renewed.

Today, I will cultivate inner peace.

As we think, so we are.

Many of us fill our minds with negative thoughts. We tell ourselves, I can't, I'm not good enough, I'm going to fail. These ideas probably come from somewhere in our past, influenced no doubt by other voices.

It's time we got rid of these self-defeating, erroneous beliefs. What we tell ourselves can undermine our self-confidence or build it up. We can practice positive reinforcement and affirm our capabilities and our worth: I may not do this perfectly, but I'm learning. I have a special contribution to make in this world. I can meet the challenges that come my way.

Affirming our good qualities, spending time with people who build us up rather than tear us down, looking at the positive side of our situation, giving ourselves credit for what we do well — little by little we increase our self-esteem. When we feel good about ourselves, we feel good about others too. The positive ripples spread, creating a healthy and productive environment.

Today, I will affirm my good qualities so they become stronger.

*You can love the body you have
now, even though it's not perfect.*

You don't have to wait until you reach a certain number of pounds to put a stamp of approval on your body. You can love and affirm it right now, just as it is, warts and all. How would it feel to forgive yourself for your physical imperfections — your crooked nose, your boniness or excess weight, whatever you don't like about the way you look? Imagine how it would feel to love and cherish your body.

Something in the back of our minds may be suspicious of the concept of self-love, fearing we would be condoning vanity or narcissism. But if we don't love ourselves, how can we love anyone else? And if we don't accept our physical components, how can we develop a healthy self-esteem?

Loving our bodies does not imply any lack of humility. We're not claiming to be more attractive than other people — we're exhibiting gratitude and appreciation for being alive. Since they will be with us as long as we live, isn't it time to make friends with our bodies right now?

*My body is mine to love and enjoy today, just as
it is.*

Honesty saves time and trouble.

How complicated we make our lives when we are less than honest with ourselves and others! Dishonesty inevitably backfires and catches up with us, and then we not only have a messy situation to untangle, we also lose our credibility.

Honesty is a cornerstone of recovery. We have probably tried to hide our eating disorder, but until we admit we have a problem, it is difficult to get better. So we become honest about what and how we eat. We stop being dishonest with food, with ourselves, and with other people. When we break through our denial, we are on the road to getting well.

As we reap the benefits of being honest about what we eat, we come to understand more fully the importance of honesty in the other areas of our lives. Ours is a comprehensive program — the Steps apply to everything we do.

Getting honest with ourselves and others makes life easier and simpler. We bring the dark corners of our lives into the light so we have nothing to hide. We no longer have to concoct stories. Our personal integrity makes us strong.

Where will honesty lead me today?

*Who are we to refuse forgiveness to
ourselves?*

Forgiveness and amends apply not only to
others but also to ourselves. Isn't it a subtle form
of pride that causes us to be unrelenting in our
self-judgment? Wallowing in guilt is a way of remaining self-centered and an excuse for inaction.
We get stuck in our bad feelings, we berate ourselves for our failings, and we cling adamantly to
a fictional standard of perfection.

This is not helpful. It feeds our eating disorder.
Since guilt is uncomfortable, we are tempted to
look for relief in the form of extra calories or
unhealthy restriction. Either way, we punish
ourselves.

Practicing forgiveness begins at home, with our
own failings, because the way we get better is by
accepting our mistakes. We can be our own best
ally, understanding the pressures and insecurities
that prompt us to turn in a less-than-stellar performance and allowing ourselves the freedom to try
again. Forgiving ourselves goes hand in hand with
forgiving others.

I can be humble enough today to forgive myself.

Yesterday is over.

It is a fact of life that what is old dies to make way for what is new. Endings are often painful — we mourn the death of a relationship, we regret leaving a familiar neighborhood, we don't like to say good-bye.

Endings, though, give us the chance to begin again. A new friend comes in to fill the empty space left when an old friend moves away. A new school, a new job, a new season of the year — these are fresh starts that evolve from what has gone before.

We need not fear the inevitable endings in our lives. Daily, we are renewed. Our bodies produce new cells continually. When we are going through an ending, we may not be able to see the new beginning that lies beyond, but we can trust it will be there for us when we are ready. We can welcome the new opportunities that each day brings and consider them gifts from the Higher Power that is with us to guide us through each end and each beginning.

I will let yesterday end so that today can begin.

How many ways can you brush your teeth?

Our habits save time, and some of the good ones, such as abstinence, can also save our lives. A fine line separates useful habits from ruts, however — the former, we wish to cultivate, and the latter, we'd just as soon avoid.

How about trying a new route to work? It might take a little longer, but you'd also have different scenery to view. How about doing some relaxing-stretching-unwinding exercises before dinner? Introducing novelty into the details of our existence makes us aware that today is a new day and that we can alter our responses.

Habits are our servants, not our masters. When we see how easy it is to change the color of our toothbrush and start with the bottom teeth instead of the top, we can branch out to other, more significant activities. We can make changes in our behavior that will change our lives in positive ways.

What would you like to do differently today? What specific action can you take to begin to climb out of an uncomfortable rut?

I will identify an unproductive habit today and turn it upside down.

*When craving strikes, what is it
really about?*

For some of us, abstinence brings complete relief from the craving we tried to satisfy with binge foods or by seriously restricting our eating. For others of us, cravings continue to strike, threatening our recovery.

There are things we can do if we are seized by an overwhelming desire for something to eat when it's not time to eat. We know that once we start eating, we may not be able to stop. We can stand back for a moment and examine the craving. We can go down deep into the desire for something sweet, something smooth, something crunchy, something creamy. We can discover what the desire is really about and if food will really satisfy it. We can learn what would satisfy it. We can learn to live with some temporary dissatisfaction in the interest of long-term health and happiness.

Our cravings for food we don't need, as well as our cravings to be thinner than is healthy, can teach us about the gaps in our lives. They can direct us to what we do need.

---

*The next time craving strikes, I will let it guide me
to a deeper understanding of what I really need.*

*When we give from the heart, we
lose nothing.*

The heart is a spiritual muscle as well as a physical one. Exercise keeps it in shape. When we give a gift from the heart, our energy is recharged, not depleted.

We can only give what we have. To be recovering is to be collecting a storehouse of gifts to share. Our program literature is full of insights that we can pass along, not only in our words but in our actions and our attitudes. Beyond what we read, we have the example of others who are also recovering and the insights we gain ourselves as we practice the principles each day.

Emotional malnutrition is a real phenomenon, and those of us who have struggled with an eating disorder are not the only sufferers. As we get better, we in turn can be agents of healing. When we reach out to others from the heart, the net result is gain for all.

The nurturing I give today will keep my heart in good shape.

*Will we risk disappointment, or will
we hide?*

No one likes to be turned down or rejected. But
if we don't ask for what we want because we're
afraid the answer will be no, we put ourselves in
a box and close the lid.

If we invite someone to a party, the person may
say no. If we ask for a raise, we may not get it. On
the other hand, if we don't make requests, we're
not likely to receive what we want and need.
Someone once said if he didn't get turned down
at least three times a day, he figured he hadn't
asked for enough.

We're big people now. If someone turns us
down, we will be disappointed but we don't need
to be crushed. And we don't need to console ourselves with extra food, or starve ourselves in an effort to be in control. The faith that we will receive
what we need gives us the confidence to ask for
it and the serenity to accept an answer that is
different from what we thought we wanted to
hear.

*I can risk disappointment today, because I be-
lieve my Higher Power's plans for me are good.*

*Friendship can be invited but not
commanded.*

We know that food is not a viable substitute for
people. We know we need friends, but some of us
aren't sure how to make them. We may have spent
years hiding from people and being self-absorbed
in our eating disorder. Soliciting friendship makes
us feel vulnerable. What if the other person
doesn't want to be our friend?

That's a chance we take. We can't command
someone to like us. All we can do is offer our genuine interest and then see what happens. There's
one thing we have going for us now — we know
the way out of isolation, because we've found a
circle of recovering people who understand
where we've been. New friendships can begin
naturally as an outgrowth of our shared recovery.

The Twelve Step philosophy changes our attitude from grasping to asking. We accept that we
cannot command God, the weather, our mother-
in-law, or anything else that crosses our path. But
as we submit our lives to the management of a
Higher Power, we are given opportunities to invite the friendship we need.

*I will invite friendship today by being genuinely
interested in someone else.*

*Recovery transforms all-or-nothing
into balance.*

Many of us have tended to think and act in terms of extremes. We fasted, or we ate everything in sight. We sat around doing nothing, or we crammed three days' worth of work into one. A friend was perfect, or he or she was hopelessly impossible. We didn't exercise at all, or we ran miles and miles.

We're learning how to introduce balance into our life so that we do not swing wildly from one extreme to the other. We need to balance activity and rest, work and play, time spent with people and time spent alone. Gradually, we find a natural rhythm that works for us. *Either/or* becomes *both/and.*

Communicating with others helps keep us in balance. Our perceptions can be distorted — when we veer too far in one direction, we need to air our views and feelings so that we get the kind of helpful feedback that corrects our course. Perfect balance is a goal that we never fully attain, but we can make progress toward it.

I am grateful for the balance of recovery

*We leave home to find out who we
are and who we can become.*

Growing up. Becoming our own person. Separating from our family of origin. This is not an easy task, but it is one that is demanded of each of us if we are to develop as an individual.

Problems with food indicate that we may not have fully accomplished the task. We may have followed a family pattern of overeating, of placing too much emphasis on food, of equating food with love, or of undereating for attention. Compulsive behavior in the area of food and eating keeps us stuck in cycles of dependency.

Some of us leave home physically but stay overly attached emotionally. Some of us move away geographically but use food to make us feel at home. An eating disorder gives us the chance to examine and reevaluate our relationships with parents and other family members. Indeed, our recovery depends on being able to separate our need for emotional nourishment from our need for food. Learning to eat for health may involve deviating from family patterns so we can become the person we want to be.

Today, I will examine where I am on my journey toward maturity.

Since this is the only body I have,
I'm taking care of it.

Our bodies are wonderfully made — and resilient. We punish them with bingeing, purging, and starving. We abuse them with alcohol, drugs, and overwork; amazingly, with recovery, they bounce back and become healthy again. But our bodies do not have an infinite recovery potential. Sooner or later, if we continue to abuse them, permanent damage occurs.

When I follow my food plan, my body functions beautifully — the way it should. I remember the physical discomfort of overeating, and I remember how weak I felt when I was dangerously restricting my intake. I don't want to go back to either extreme, not when I know how good moderation makes me feel.

I respect and cherish my body as my Higher Power's gift to me. With the gift goes the responsibility to care for it, to nourish and nurture it with the right amounts of the right kind of food, exercise, and rest.

My body deserves my care and attention today.

*Acknowledging anger helps us get
rid of it.*

Denying or repressing anger rarely works. Sooner or later the anger comes out. It may come out indirectly (you're mad at your partner but yell at your son), or it may be internalized (you deny your anger and become depressed). Those of us with eating disorders often act out the anger either by bingeing or by not eating enough.

Becoming aware of anger is the first step toward dealing with it. We need to know how it feels to be angry, and we need to stay with the feeling long enough to learn what is triggering it: Am I mad at my partner? Did he or she do something that reminded me of a controlling parent? We then have to figure out if we're overreacting or if we have a legitimate grievance. Finally we need to decide what we're going to do with our anger.

Once identified, anger can be expressed and released. Perhaps all we need to do is express it to ourselves, an understanding listener, or an empty chair. Maybe we need to confront the person with whom we are angry. After acknowledging and expressing the anger, we can turn it over to a Higher Power and be rid of it.

Am I trying to hide angry feelings?

*Experience is easier to digest in
small bites than in large ones.*

When we worry about future events, we're asking for emotional indigestion. How much effort
we waste when we try, through worry, to control
future happenings!

When we stay in the present, our experience
unfolds gradually, bit by bit, in manageable
proportions. Coping with actual situations is far
easier than trying to handle imaginary ones. Our
Higher Power gives us strength for today's tasks
and pleasures. We can believe that when tomorrow comes, we'll have new energy for tomorrow's challenges.

When we focus on now, just now, we discover
that our ability to deal with current experience
surprises us. We are fully adequate to the demands of the moment, since in the present we
have access to a Power greater than our own.

*Today, I will digest actual experience as it hap-
pens — in small pieces.*

June

*Abstinence gives our spirit room to
grow.*

If we eat too much, if we're continually preoccupied with the material things of life — food,
clothing, shelter, and possessions — we run the
risk of spiritual starvation. But if we don't eat
enough, we're also limiting our potential for
spiritual growth.

Feed the body, yes. Feed it reasonable amounts
of nutritious food. Take care of other material
needs also, but not to the point where an obsession to acquire more and more interferes with the
life of the spirit. Allow for some emptiness so
there is room for unexpected gifts.

The fewer our needs, the freer we are. When
we're not bogged down with excess food, a compulsion to be too thin, or too much concern about
how we look and what we possess, then our
heart, mind, and spirit are free to expand. We are
able to live life to its fullest.

*Today's abstinence keeps my spirit alive and
well.*

*Reducing the excess baggage of
things we "have to have and do"
makes our journey more pleasant.*

Traveling light — do we know how? Do we want to practice making today's trip easier and more enjoyable?

The fewer things we put on our "must have and must do" list, the freer we are. Do we really "have to have" excess food, which produces excess weight, slows us down, and makes us uncomfortable in body and in psyche? Do we "have to" overachieve to the point where we drive ourselves beyond reasonable expectations at school, at work, in sports, or other activities? Do we "have to have" things we cannot realistically afford?

Having to have a lot and having to do a lot creates stress and tension. Let's examine our list of today's activities and see if crossing off some of the items would make today's journey more satisfying and pleasurable.

Is there something I think I have to have or do today that needs to be re-evaluated and perhaps discarded?

Celebrate by feeling good.

We know what makes us feel good: following a food plan, getting enough rest and exercise, sharing love with family and friends, having useful work to do and interesting activities to enjoy, feeding our spirit, being of service to others.

When we are tempted to neglect any of these, we need to think about the results. What good is a so-called celebration if we feel terrible the next day? Throwing our hard-won discipline out the window may have a powerful short-term appeal, but what about the long-range consequences? We know what those are — we know how we will feel tomorrow if we binge or starve today.

We are blessed with a program that nurtures us physically, emotionally, and spiritually. We know where the answers are. Let's not get sidetracked into thinking that abandoning our program "just this once" will make us feel good. We know better!

I celebrate today by following my program and feeling good.

*We don't want to live in the past,
but we do need to learn to live comfortably with it.*

"We will not regret the past nor wish to shut the door on it."* This is a promise of the Twelve Step program.

One of the most useful tools we have for learning to live with our past is the Fourth Step inventory. Once we have examined our dark corners and shared with someone else the times when we did not live up to our expectations, we no longer fear reminders of those times, nor do we try to block them out with food.

It takes energy to try to hold shut the door to the past. Coming to terms with mistakes we have made, making amends, forgiving ourselves, and forgiving others releases this energy so we can use it for living more fully now, in the present. Allowing the door to the past to swing open in its own time gives us access to the good memories that we were also repressing.

Is there something I need to do today so that I can live more comfortably with the past?

---

* *Alcoholics Anonymous* (New York: Alcoholics Anonymous World Services, Inc. 1955), 83.

Misery is optional.

We may have learned to be miserable, but we can choose to unlearn it. Though we can't control what happens to us, we can determine how we will interpret and react to what happens. We can moan about the things we don't like, using them as excuses for self-pity ("poor me"), or we can implement the Serenity Prayer, accepting what we can't change and changing what we can.

In the past, we often made ourselves miserable by overeating, by bingeing and purging, by self-starvation. Now, how often do we continue to invite misery by thinking we ought to be able to control other people? What part do unrealistic expectations play in the creation and continuation of our misery?

When we're hurting, we need to do something about it. A physical hurt may require a doctor, an emotional pain may call for a therapist or friend, and spiritual distress may indicate the need for more prayer and meditation, closer contact with a Higher Power. We can accept responsibility for our feelings, become willing to go to any lengths to get well, and choose not to be miserable.

Responding with misery is not on my list of options for today.

We can choose to bloom where we're planted.

We're not always where we want to be. Frequently, the conditions and demands of reality place us somewhere other than the spot we would have preferred. Perhaps because of family considerations, job circumstances, or financial constraints, we find ourselves physically located in one place but mentally wishing we were somewhere else.

Our concentration and attention become divided, and we feel frustrated. Since we don't want to turn to food to relieve the frustration, what are we going to do?

If circumstances are beyond our power to change, or if we choose not to change them because of values that are important to us, our best response is to accept where we are and focus our attention on the here and now. Since our lives are in the hands of a Higher Power, we can be assured we are situated exactly where we are supposed to be. Our task is to be fully awake and aware of present reality so we can learn what we need to from this stage of our life journey.

Today, I will strive to be fully present and contribute my best, wherever I am.

*When the well threatens to run dry,
it's time to rest and refill.*

We can't always be doing and giving and producing. There comes a time when we run out of steam, and that's when we need to know how to replenish our supply of energy and enthusiasm.

Some of us get recharged by being with other people. Some of us need to be quiet and alone. All of us can profit from an inspirational uplift, whether it comes from music, something we read, a conversation with a friend, savoring the beauty of nature, or a period of meditation.

Vacations can be wonderful, but we're not always able to take them when we need them. What we can do is learn how to create for ourselves islands of recreation — *re-creation* — which may be inserted into our busy, everyday schedule. We can learn to stop and refill the well before it runs dry, so we do not drive ourselves into the kind of exhaustion that threatens recovery.

I will build an island of re-creation *into today's schedule.*

Steady progress wears better than overachievement.

"Easy does it, but do it" is one of the slogans from the Twelve Step program. We don't expect ourselves to perform exceptional feats. It was that kind of thinking — when we decided we had to be the best, or the thinnest, or the most perfect — that fed our eating disorder.

The goals of recovery are more realistic. We don't have to be perfect or the best, but we do expect to make progress, one day at a time. Progress comes naturally as we devote our attention to the Steps of the program. Some days we may not see visible signs of forward motion, but if we are doing the footwork — getting to meetings, making telephone calls, working the Steps — we're eventually going to see results.

Overachievement was a tightrope that we walked with dread. Steady progress is a path that requires sincere effort and dedication, but one that we walk with confidence, since we are able to stay on it. We each proceed at our own pace, guided and supported each step of the way by the God of our understanding.

Today, I will strive for progress, not perfection.

Is it love, or is it addiction?

As we recover from an eating disorder, we are vulnerable to getting lost in a relationship, or in a series of relationships. We are moving away from being addicted to overeating, purging, or compulsive dieting, and there is a danger that we may transfer the obsession and the dependency to a person or persons. In place of eating behavior that is hazardous to our health, we can substitute one or more hazardous attachments. We do not want to do this.

The principles of the program serve us well as we move away from being obsessed with food and diets and seek to form relationships that promote our physical, emotional, and spiritual well-being. If we stay grounded in the Steps, in contact with a Higher Power, in communication with understanding friends and our own inner voice, we are less likely to lose ourselves in an addictive love relationship.

We need special people in our lives. We need to give and receive love. We also need to maintain our self-esteem and individual boundaries so that our love is strong and healthy.

May I learn to love without losing myself.

If I find myself in an uncomfortable situation today, I need to decide whether to stay or leave.

As recovery moves me closer to myself, I am more attuned to the internal cues that prompt my behavior. Formerly, if I were uncomfortable, perhaps because I was with people who were not the best companions for me, I would feel the inner unrest, but try to make it go away with food. Now that unnecessary food is no longer an option, I must find another way of dealing with uncomfortable situations.

If there's no good reason to stay around people I feel uneasy with, I will find a way to leave. If I have important reasons for remaining, I need to analyze the psychic cost to me and determine if the reasons for remaining are worth the cost. If they are, I will stay. But I will be aware of my inner feelings and acknowledge them instead of burying them in food.

No matter what the situation, and whether I stay or leave, I can learn from the experience and maintain my abstinence.

My decision to stay in, or leave, an uncomfortable situation will not affect my abstinence today.

Expect to be surprised.

No matter how diligently we try, we can't make life behave the way we think it ought to. Our best predictions for how we think life will go often miss the mark.

The things we worry about frequently do not materialize, and our actual problems often come as complete surprises. We may attempt to create an illusion of control, using food, weight, and diets as elements we can manipulate, but, in reality, we do not control the events of our lives.

What we can influence is how we respond to the unexpected. We can hold ourselves ready and prepared to make the most of whatever situation arises. Of course, pleasant surprises are easier to handle than unpleasant ones, but we may miss them if we don't have the flexibility to appreciate and enjoy them when they beckon.

An attitude of trust, the belief that life is good, and the confidence that a Higher Power is on our side keep us prepared and ready to meet the challenges of the unexpected.

The surprises today brings are life's gift to me. How I respond is my gift to life.

Conflict can produce positive results.

If our policy is to avoid conflict at all cost, we may impede our growth by trying to sweep important issues under the rug and refusing to deal with them. The issues don't disappear, however, and by sweeping them under the rug, we make them more toxic and unwieldy.

Conflict is bound to occur in any vital, important relationship, and the question is how to handle it. Allowing conflict to be brought into the open usually makes it much more manageable than trying to ignore it. If there's fear of conflict, we're less likely to feel free to be ourselves.

Since I don't want to use destructive eating patterns as an escape from conflict, I'd like to find a better solution. When I am willing to talk about what's bothering me, to state my position and listen to yours, to ask for help from a Higher Power, it's very possible that we will reach an understanding that enhances our relationship. Conflict does not need to destroy. Using the Steps, we can build on our differences and both come out stronger.

If I find myself in a situation of conflict today, I will try working through it rather than attempting to avoid it.

Are you as insecure as I am?

I look at you on the outside, and you seem to "have it all together." You appear to know who you are, what you want, and how to go about the business of living. In contrast, when I look at myself, I am painfully aware of my insides, which are often confused and unsure.

One of the important benefits of belonging to a support group is that we can express our uncertainties and insecurities in a safe, understanding environment. We hear other people express the feelings we thought we had to hide. We learn we are not alone in our anxiety, embarrassment, frustration, and lack of control.

If you, too, have feelings of inadequacy, then I don't need to put up a false front with you. I can be myself and join the human race. I discover that I am not unique, that you share my problems, and that together we can find solutions.

As I give understanding and support today, support and understanding will come back to me.

In case of emergency, let go.

Strange advice. When crisis threatens, all of our instincts urge us to hang on tight to whatever is close at hand and does not move. We make contingency plans, take out insurance policies, and cling to our security systems.

It's possible, however, that the props to which we cling will prevent us from moving out of the crisis situation. If my house were on fire, I would not want to barricade myself inside. If I were on a sinking ship, it would be foolish to strap myself into a bunk.

Yet this is often the type of behavior we exhibit when we feel threatened and buffeted by unexpected events. We hang on to old systems of response, including overeating and undereating, instead of trusting a Higher Power to lead us to safety. When we let go of our inadequate ways of handling stress and avail ourselves of our spiritual resources, we are given the strength we need to meet the crisis.

In case of an emergency today, I will let go and allow myself to be guided by my Higher Power.

Not every day is a picnic, but there's always something to be learned.

Some mornings you may wonder how you will ever get through the day. Maybe you have something to do that you've been dreading and putting off. Perhaps you have to be somewhere you'd rather not be. Or, you might simply be at a low point in your life, wondering where your path is leading.

Even though we're not in charge of the big picture, we can believe that the details of each day fit the way they should. Some days, we need to remind ourselves that all we have to do is put one foot in front of the other and proceed according to our best information and ability. The difficult experiences teach us valuable lessons.

When our attitude is one of willingness to learn, we stop sitting around waiting to be amused and indulged, and we roll up our sleeves for the challenges of the day. Each step we take brings us further along on the pathway of recovery.

What will today's events teach me about recovery?

*Flexibility is an asset we can
develop.*

Does the rigidity of self-will ever get in our way?
Most of us would probably answer yes. We have
compulsively tried to make things go our way, es-
tablishing standards and timetables to which we
expected the rest of the world to conform. Then,
when self-will didn't work, we have become frustrated and unhappy.

Letting go of self-will is a major part of recovering from an eating disorder or any other kind of
compulsive behavior. We learn that we can function even if life does not proceed according to our
timetable. We develop trust in a Higher Power's
plan, which allows us to be comfortably flexible.
We learn to live and let live, to permit others to
have the same freedom we want for ourselves.

Being flexible brings new options. We become
open to possibilities we hadn't considered; we
have a wider range of choices. Best of all, we escape the tyranny of self-will.

*Today, I will be open and flexible so that I may
take advantage of new possibilities.*

Whatever our weight, we can be kind.

It's not necessary to have perfect proportions in order to have friends. We don't need to put off being good to people until some magic moment in the future when our bodies look exactly the way we'd like them to. Right now, we can be valued and loved for who we are inside and for the kind and thoughtful way we treat others.

We can be sensitive to the needs and desires of family, friends, co-workers, and acquaintances without compromising to the point where we lose our own boundaries. When we fully accept ourselves as we are, we can be generous with other people. With a firm grounding in a Power greater than ourselves, we can move beyond the demands of self-will and consider the well-being of those around us.

Abstinence helps us normalize our eating and maintain a healthy weight. The Steps lead us beyond the issues of food, pounds, and proportions, to the development of healthy relationships. Wherever we are on the path to normal weight, we can cultivate our ability to be good to those we love.

The kindness I share with others today will enhance my recovery.

*Human relations are an ongoing
adventure.*

Meeting new people. Rediscovering old friends. Exploring the heights and depths of intimacy. Each significant contact we make with a fellow human being opens us both to adventure. We give and we take, and with the interaction comes growth and change.

Recovery gives us the confidence to branch out and try new ways of responding. Before, we may have limited our circle of friends to those few people with whom we felt safe. Now we can seek new friendships and revitalize old ones. We can be vulnerable and risk rejection, since we like ourselves better and have the support of our program and a Higher Power.

We make mistakes. We say the wrong thing. We do something hurtful. Because we're not hiding from other people in food and diets, we are more sensitive now, quicker to say "I'm sorry," and better able to make amends. The adventure continues, as each day we learn more about relating to someone else.

May I not be afraid to reach out to those who cross my path today.

We need goals, but isn't the journey
more important than the destination?

If we're too focused on where we're going, on the outcome of our efforts and activities, we may miss the abundance life holds for us along the way. The cycle of life renews itself — we get up every morning and meet a day fresh with opportunities.

We set goals and make plans, but when we turn our will and our lives over to the God of our understanding, we prepare ourselves to welcome the unexpected, the creative, the serendipitous.

Our ultimate destination is hidden in the future. What we can see clearly is today's path. Let's give today's experience our full attention; let's keep our minds and bodies in the best possible condition for the journey. Careful execution of the steps along the way ensures that we will be pleased with the destination.

Today is important. I will pay careful attention to the details of my journey and prepare myself to travel in the best possible condition.

*Trading old habits for new life is
what recovery is all about.*

It's time to let go of the old patterns that no longer serve our new selves. What we may have relied on in the past — excess food, chemicals, dependent relationships, compulsive exercise — is no longer the focal point of our existence. Now that we are recovering, we have access to much more effective help through a source of power greater than ourselves.

Tapping into a spiritual source of strength makes it possible for us to shed the patterns that blocked our progress. We don't need them anymore. We don't need excess food, harmful chemicals, or dependent relationships, and we don't need to starve our bodies in search of a magic shape. Our Higher Power has other plans for us.

Recognizing we are part of the stream of goodness in this world, we can let go of whatever impedes our growth. Recovery promises new life; recovery *is* new life. What we do is turn over the old habits so we are open to the new life our Higher Power offers us each day.

I will be open to new possibilities and new life today.

Say yes to love.

We want to feel loved. For many of us, the connection between food and love has been a powerful one, and so we associated the feeling of a full stomach with the feeling of being loved. But something was missing, and we mistakenly thought more food might be the answer. Others of us thought we could become deserving of the love we sought by reaching an ideal state of thinness.

There is a better, healthier, more direct way of receiving the love we need. We receive love by giving it, by saying yes to the opportunities we have every day to make a loving overture, a loving response. To wait until some future time when we might be more perfect, or the other person more deserving, is to miss today's chance.

When we say yes to love, we affirm that we are valuable and have something to offer, and we affirm someone else as worthy of receiving our care and concern. The inner satisfaction we experience feeds our heart's hunger and nurtures our recovery.

My actions today will say yes to love.

*When we don't feel serene, we can
act as if we do.*

Emotional ups and downs are a fact of life, but
we can choose how we will respond to them. We
can get lost in anger, panic, and irritability, or we
can cultivate an inner center of serenity to which
we can retreat when emotional storms are raging.

When we are upset, we can remember that this
storm, too, shall pass, and that in a few hours or
a few days we may hardly recall what it was all
about. Even in the middle of the storm, we can appear serene. We can act calmly, speak softly and
slowly, breathe deeply, and our emotions will get
the message.

The more we practice serenity, the more it becomes a habit. Being willing to give up control
and trust a Higher Power is the price we pay to be
serene. When we're willing to try it, we find it's
worth the cost.

---

*Just for today, I am willing to give up the illusion
of control in exchange for a measure of serenity.*

*Recovery gives us the opportunity to
become whole.*

Integrity, wholeness, health — this is what we
want. The work of recovery is to integrate the
various parts of ourselves that are in conflict, to
unite our instincts, desires, thoughts, beliefs, feelings, and actions so that we are a harmonious
whole.

This is a large order, an undertaking that we
never fully complete, since we are evolving,
changing personalities. One day at a time, we're
learning. We find out which actions are compati-
ble with our goals and beliefs, how our instincts
can serve rather than betray us, how our minds,
hearts, and bodies can work together without
fighting each other.

How do we do this? By surrendering our fighting inner factions to the gentle guidance of a
Higher Power. By seeking earnestly and diligently
to know our Higher Power's will for us. By trying
what seems right, and if that doesn't work, by going back for further direction and trying again.
The reward is worth the effort!

*Today, may I come closer to being the whole per-
son I am meant to be.*

Daily, we determine our priorities.

Priorities are not merely something we establish once a year, once a month, or even once a week. Our priorities are visible in the myriad decisions we make and actions we take each day.

Being closely in touch with our inner selves and our Higher Power helps assure that our priorities reflect our genuine needs and desires. When we are securely centered, we will not be unduly influenced by other people but will know what is truly important to us and necessary for our health and well-being.

We set our priorities when we do our grocery shopping and plan our meals. We set them when we choose between playing tennis or reading a book or going to see a friend. We set them when we decide how to respond to a negative comment from a co-worker. Our daily priorities reflect who we are and determine what we are becoming. Let's set them with care.

Today, may I put first things first.

*If we are willing to go to any
lengths, we shall recover.*

The fact that we have come to a structured program and are trying it is a good sign. It means we
have recognized our need for help and acknowledged that our own solutions were not
working.

Recovery requires that we determine how far
we are willing to go to get better. It requires that
we often give up doing things our way. We may
have to rearrange our schedules and follow someone else's suggestions about what, when, and
how much we eat. We will almost certainly have
to consider revealing our weak points to strangers
and to entertain the possibility of belief and trust
in a Higher Power. We may have to decide
whether to make major changes in our lifestyle if
it is unhealthy or to give up a relationship that
doesn't fill our needs. Above all, recovery will
mean that we keep trying in spite of setbacks.

The path of recovery is a demanding one. To
stay on it, we must be rigorously honest and dare
to give up whatever makes us weaker in favor of
what makes us stronger. We can follow the directions and proceed toward our destination.

Today, and every day, my goal is recovery.

The gifts we receive are meant to be shared.

Thanks to the progress I am making in recovery, I like to think I am more loving, more open, more spontaneous, more confident. I believe these gifts have come to me through my Higher Power, the Twelve Steps, and the friends who have helped me grow.

If I am to keep the gifts, I must share them. They are mine as long as I give them away. To do that I need to realize we're all working toward a similar goal: that of developing our potential and becoming who we are meant to be. We help each other toward this goal by sharing our experience, strength, and hope.

Close, warm, loving contacts with my family and friends are what feed my heart and spirit and fill the inner emptiness that no amount of excess food or dangerous weight loss can fill. When I am willing to share the gifts I have received, I always have enough, because what I give comes back to me.

I will take advantage of today's opportunities for caring and sharing, remembering that my recovery depends not on what I have but on what I give.

The best way to get help is to ask for it.

Help is available, but we need to ask for it. If we're lost, we can ask for directions. If the furnace stops working, we can call someone who knows how to repair it. If we are emotionally upset, we can talk to a friend or a professional counselor who can help us find a way out of the difficulty.

Admitting we need help is the first step toward recovery. An eating disorder is a sign that we have chronic problems that need attention. We are learning ways of working directly on these problems instead of compulsively covering them up with food, diets, or exercise.

We are not alone. We have a support group. We have friends. We have community resources, therapists, and counselors who can help. We have a Power greater than ourselves that we contact through our relationships with other people and during the time we spend in quiet meditation.

I will be humble enough today to ask for help when I need it.

*If it's really good, it's worth the
wait.*

Knowing what we want and being willing to
work and wait for it — surely these are among
recovery's greatest blessings. Letting go of addictive behavior gives us the freedom to discover
what it is we really want, what will satisfy our
deepest hunger. Curbing our impulsiveness enables us to work toward long-term goals and wait
for their fruition.

Often, the work needs to be done on ourselves
— preparing ourselves in mind, body, and spirit
to receive the good things life has in store for us.
Taken conscientiously, the Twelve Steps prepare
us for better relationships, more effective functioning at work or school, and a more abundant
spiritual life.

When we don't insist on having what we think
we want, and having it yesterday, our options expand. We can choose to pass up a temporary high
in favor of a lasting benefit. We can wait for what
promises long-term satisfaction, trusting it will
come to us if we're supposed to have it.

*I will work on my attitude today, enjoying what
I have and expecting good things to come.*

We can open ourselves to receive the wisdom of the body.

There's a good chance that we are not fully in tune with our bodies. When we were starving ourselves or bingeing, we didn't know when our bodies had had too little or too much food. Now, we may not know if we've had enough rest, exercise, or sensual pleasure. We may not know what our bodies are telling us when they seem opposed to what our minds are thinking.

The body has a wisdom that is both ancient and immediate. It is where we live, and we can become attuned to the messages it sends. If we do not, we risk being divided.

We connect with the wisdom of the body by paying close attention to how we really feel, as opposed to how others think we should feel or how we might like to feel. We observe our physical reactions nonjudgmentally, since acceptance is a prerequisite for making positive changes.

Recovery puts us at peace with our bodies. We accept their needs and limitations; we enjoy their pleasures. Understanding our bodies' messages helps us avoid relapse and cultivate serenity.

Today, I will be aware of and receptive to the wisdom of my body.

Life has more to offer than food and diets.

Before we began the process of recovering from our eating disorder, many of us could not remember a time when we weren't desperately trying to lose weight. Even if our weight was within a normal range, we may have thought we needed to be thinner, and we probably feared the next binge that would push us back into being unacceptable. How constricted we were — obsessed with calories and ounces and how much is enough.

Food and diets are never enough. We need much more, and thanks to the blessings of recovery, we are finding what we need. Today, we can plan and eat three moderate meals and spend the rest of the time exploring and enjoying the other good things that life offers us. We can talk to a friend, take up a new hobby, organize a closet, listen to music, figure out a more effective way of getting a job done, take a walk and look at the stars. We can do something for someone else. Our horizons are expanding.

Today, I will take time to explore and enjoy a new benefit of recovery.

July

Deciding to want what we have is a giant step in the direction of having enough.

Sometimes we honestly do not have enough. We may not have enough money to pay the rent, or enough food to feed our family, or enough self-esteem to act in our own best interest, or enough caring from the people around us to make us feel loved. These are real, legitimate needs, and we may require help to fill them.

Sometimes, though, our wants are so unrealistic that what we do have gets pushed aside and ignored. Do we really need a bigger house? A fancier car? A second helping? A new man or woman in our life?

We can decide that what we have today is enough for today. We can trust that if we do the work we need to do each day, we will also have enough for tomorrow. We can spend a few moments right now cataloging a portion of the material and spiritual goods that are ours today.

When I decide to want what I have, I begin to know how it feels to have enough.

*One thing is certain — we will have
ups and downs.*

We can accept the challenge of taking life
straight, without trying to medicate ourselves
with food, or control our feelings through self-
starvation. This way, we become open to good
feelings as well as painful ones. We experience joy
along with sadness.

We would like to make the good feelings last, to
stay on a permanent high. In the past, we may
have tried to do this with food, chemicals, or
compulsive activity, but sooner or later what
went up came down, perhaps with a resounding
thud. We cannot have permanent highs, but
through our program of recovery, we can learn to
function through highs, lows, and in between.

When we accept downs as well as ups, we gain
a perspective that softens the sharp edges of extremes. Whether we are emotionally up or down
at a given moment, we can maintain the inner
peace and serenity that comes from developing
our spiritual selves.

My spirit can handle the ups and downs of today.

*It's easier to say I'm sorry than risk
a binge.*

When we get angry, we say and do things that hurt other people. Sometimes we unintentionally hurt those we care about through lack of attention or insensitivity to their needs. However it happens, we undoubtedly cause harm by what we say and do and by what we fail to say and do.

We have a plan of action to follow when this happens. We can apologize and make amends to the best of our ability. Saying I'm sorry may not be easy, particularly if we tend to dwell on the other person's role in the conflict rather than on our own. Most likely, both people have made mistakes, but ours are the only ones for which we can apologize.

Making a genuine attempt to clear the air and restore harmony is infinitely preferable to letting anger and resentment fester and push us back into unhealthy habits.

---

*When I am wrong today, may I promptly admit
my error.*

Recovery sets us free.

Freedom is what recovery is all about. Not only are we free from addictive behavior and food abuse, but we are free to become who we are and enjoy all that life has to offer. We may not hear bands playing and see fireworks every day, but we will know a new dimension of peace and serenity.

Although recovery does not guarantee freedom from pain and distress, it promises us greater resources for coping with trouble. With the help of abstinence and the Twelve Steps, we become free to work toward resolving our difficulties instead of escaping into false solutions.

We must remain strong and guard the freedom that comes with abstinence. Whatever threatens abstinence should be avoided: we don't want to transfer the food obsession to something else, such as drugs, compulsive shopping, or addictive relationships. To remain free, we stay in touch with others who are also recovering and with the Higher Power that guides and supports us.

I will celebrate my freedom today and every day.

How much exercise is enough?

For some of us, recovering means more exercise, and for others, it means less. We need to move our bodies — the question is, how much?

Those of us who have become sedentary will start slowly and gradually increase our level of activity so that our metabolic rate will rise and we will burn calories more efficiently. Exercise helps us get back in shape and enjoy our bodies. If we have been compulsively overexercising, we will reduce our activity to a healthful level.

Not too much, not too little. Moderation applies to exercise as well as food. The right amount helps us relax, avoid depression, and feel more energetic. We can arrive at a plan that suits our individual requirements and preferences. We are reclaiming our bodies, and exercise makes us feel good.

I will plan time today for enjoyable exercise and movement — the right amount for me.

*The more fully we share our
thoughts, feelings, and experiences,
the more we learn from them.*

Other people help us define and validate our opinions, emotions, and reactions. In the process of thinking out loud, describing my feelings, or experiencing an event with a friend, I can often learn more than I would have by myself. I discover feelings I didn't know I had, I see possibilities that previously had not occurred to me, and I am aware of details I might have missed.

We are blessed indeed when we have friends who care about us, who listen to what we have to say, and who accept us as we are. If we have found it difficult to trust other people in the past, we may need to make a conscious effort to cultivate the kind of friendship that gives us the support we crave. What we find is that people treat us pretty much as we treat them — if we are open, sincere, and accepting, we will attract the same kind of behavior in return.

We are learning that the more of ourselves we share with others, the more we get back in return and the more we learn.

I will share a part of myself today that was previously hidden.

Give yourself permission to play.

Life is real, life is earnest, but life is also fun. Since any obsession or addiction gradually encroaches on leisure time and eats it up, what starts as an attempt to produce pleasure can eventually have the opposite effect. Recovery gives us back the time and inclination to play.

Those of us who have forgotten how to enjoy our leisure hours have a treat in store for us. We can give ourselves permission to discover how to have fun. Often this will mean doing things with people we like to be with, but we can also have fun by ourselves. When was the last time you allowed yourself to spend an entire day doing exactly what you wanted?

Recovering means balancing our hours of work with periods of rest and play. It means learning what we like to do and letting our imagination carry us into a world of delight. It means giving expression to the child within who is always ready to have fun.

Today I will make time for fun and play.

*Do we like and enjoy our friends or
do we use them?*

With each step we take toward recovery, we gain new insight into our ways of relating to other people. With the Fourth Step inventory, we begin a process of focusing on how we can turn our weaknesses into strengths. We gain a new awareness of our motives, and we become willing to consider making changes if we see that self-will is hampering our relationships.

We realize that attempting to control other people and use them to suit our purposes does not lead to healthy give and take. We want to be strong enough so we can allow the people we love to be themselves. We want to choose our friends on the basis of compatibility, not because we expect them to fill a deficiency we see in ourselves.

Love and respect cannot be commanded. They can only be freely offered and freely returned. Genuine liking is a solid basis for friendship. Now that we are learning to like and respect — and, yes, even love — ourselves, we can relate to other people from a position of inner strength.

I will spend a few moments today evaluating my relationships.

*Daily we nurture our spiritual
awakening.*

The spiritual awakening that comes with practicing the Twelve Steps rarely happens once and
for all. For most of us, awareness of life's spiritual
dimension continues to grow as we maintain our
recovery. As we recover from food abuse, we
learn to rely on a Higher Power, and we learn to
open ourselves to spiritual gifts daily.

When we wake up abstinent and clearheaded,
we can hear birds sing, and we can feel energy and
joy. When our thoughts are not obsessed with
food, diets, and weight, we can listen to the wisdom of our inner voice.

Spiritual growth requires time, attention, and
daily discipline. We feed our spirits by reading in-
spiring and uplifting literature, by emptying our
minds and centering ourselves in quiet meditation, and by acting according to our best insights,
difficult as that may sometimes be. We nurture
our spiritual awakening by making it a priority,
the most important part of our lives.

I will nurture my spirit today.

*Acting on our spiritual motivation
brings us to the right place.*

Each of us has an inner drive to realize our potential. Our job is to uncover the drive and learn what we really want to do, whether we're speaking in terms of a lifelong career or plans for this afternoon. Our path becomes clear, one step at a time, as we follow the promptings of heart and spirit, focusing on what we can do rather than on what we cannot.

We're using our motivation to fuel our recovery. Since we want to get well, we become aware of how to operate with the support and guidance of a Power greater than ourselves. When our motivation is linked to that source of strength, we can accomplish our realistic goals. We can learn to eat three moderate meals a day, we can perform useful functions with our inborn talents and abilities, and we can live in peace and harmony with those around us.

I will take time today to notice where my spiritual motivation is directing me.

*Are you meeting roadblocks to
recovery?*

A *disorder* means out of order, not the way
things should be. Are we convinced that addictive
behavior toward food is counter to the way we
are intended to function? Or do we harbor, somewhere in the back of our minds, the idea that we'll
never change our habits?

Fear of change, unwillingness to change, and
lack of confidence in our ability to change are all
roadblocks to recovery. Believing in our capabilities is the first step toward clearing those roadblocks and realizing our potential in recovery.

Somewhere along the line we developed an eating disorder, but we don't have to be under its
power forever. We can think about what a Higher
Power would want for us, and we can decide to
move toward that positive goal.

The roadblocks of fear, unwillingness, and lack
of confidence will give way as we immerse ourselves in the Twelve Step program. We need help,
and we have help. We give help, and we receive
it. Changing to constructive habits may be slow
sometimes, but it's always possible.

---

*If I'm faced with a roadblock today, I will call on
my spiritual resources.*

Tastes change, and it's a good thing they do!

Eating is a habit, and we learn to like what we eat. If we habitually eat junk food, we learn to like junk food. If we eat nutritious food regularly, that's what we learn to like. It's amazing how much sweeter natural fruit tastes when we don't eat refined sugar!

Many of us have slipped and eaten one of our favorite foods from our bingeing days only to discover we really don't enjoy eating it anymore. But it certainly isn't necessary to have a slip in order to see if our tastes have changed. One of the advantages of being in a program of recovery is that we do not have to reinvent the wheel but can profit from other people's experiences.

The longer we maintain abstinence and eat the kind of food that makes us feel good, the better we like it and the less tempted we are by so-called "treats." We are re-educating our tastes, and the results include a healthier body and greater serenity.

Today, I will practice choosing and liking the foods that make me feel good.

•JULY 13•

Recovery leads to acceptance of greater responsibility.

Our eating disorder may have been a way of avoiding responsibility. In recovery, we discover how our disorder affected the important relationships in our lives, and we come to see how we have changed now that we are committed to the Steps.

In the process of recovery, we realize that we are working on becoming more responsible. No longer do we have the excuse of feeling so terrible from bingeing, so lightheaded from undereating, or so exhausted from exercising compulsively, that we can't cope.

As I recover, I realize that I am responsible for my thoughts, feelings, and behavior. I am responsible for seeking to know my Higher Power's will for me and to carry it out. I am learning how to deal with problems by identifying them and defining my area of responsibility. I know I can ask for the help I need, and I can acknowledge that a Power greater than myself is in charge of what lies beyond my control.

May I turn to my Higher Power today for a greater understanding of what I'm responsible for and what I cannot control.

Today's challenges contain the lessons we need to learn.

To believe in a Higher Power is to trust that our lives have purpose and meaning, that events don't happen randomly but are part of a coherent pattern.

Looking back, we see how the pieces of our experience fit together. If today, when we are presented with what may appear to be an inconvenient, if not absurd, situation, we can have faith that it is part of a larger, meaningful plan.

We may not like what's going on. We may be in circumstances that are tough to handle. We may feel sad. But, since in Step Three we have turned our will and our lives over to the care of a Power greater than ourselves, we can be confident that today's challenges are for our growth. Time may be required before we fully understand the lessons in today's events and see what they are teaching us. Even so, we can accept the challenges in good faith and meet them with inner strength. We can be willing to grow along spiritual lines.

I will accept today's challenges as lessons I need to learn.

Together we are strong.

We could not find the way to recovery alone, but together we are making progress. Most of us need all the help we can get — help from family, friends, professional counselors, and other people who can be resources for our growth. The wider and broader our support network, the stronger we are.

We hope we have moved beyond the false pride that induced us to think we had to "go it alone." When we're caught in that mind-set, asking for assistance becomes incredibly difficult. There is no logical reason to place ourselves apart from the rest of humanity, to consider ourselves so different that no one else could possibly understand our situation.

Humility opens the door for help. We become willing to join with others who are recovering, to ask for the assistance we need. Do we need to make a phone call right now? Possibly there is someone who needs the contact as much as we. The telephone is our lifeline. If we're tempted to abandon our food plan, let's call for help instead.

Today, I will remember that help is as close as my telephone.

*Trying to ignore our worries only
pushes them underground.*

Pretending we are not anxious when we are is
a tactic that fools no one, especially not ourselves.
Attempting to deny or repress our fears and worries does not work. The result is often depression
or a physical ailment, indicating that in our sub-
conscious, we know very well that something is
wrong.

The rigorous honesty of the Twelve Step way
of life saves us from playing destructive games
with ourselves. A worry that we can define and
examine in the light of day is far less threatening
than one we are trying to hide.

So let's ask ourselves what it is we fear. If our
worry is a rational one, we need to decide what
we can do to prepare for the worst-case scenario.
If the worry is irrational, we need to figure out
how to get rid of it. But, no matter whether a
worry is rational or irrational, we can't turn it over
until we acknowledge we have it. Getting our
worries out in the open and talking about them
with people whose judgment we trust keeps us
grounded in reality.

*If I am worried about something today, I will
consciously examine it so that I can resolve it.*

We're not given more than we can handle.

Sometimes I take on more than I can comfortably manage — that's one of the ways in which my life becomes unmanageable. It happens when I'm operating according to self-will rather than the will of a Higher Power.

I believe that God does not expect more of me than I can produce, that along with the challenges and difficulties I encounter comes the strength I need to cope with them and learn from them. When chaos threatens, I'm either taking on more than I should, or I'm not using the resources available to me.

With recovery, we learn to arrange our priorities so that we do not get worn out with compulsive activity and busyness. Everything becomes more manageable when we're not trying to run the show by ourselves. Solid experience teaches us that support is always at hand, that our Higher Power comes through for us when we ask for help.

I will face today's tasks, confident that I will be given the ability to accomplish my Higher Power's will for me.

*Don't miss out on today's learning
experiences.*

They won't come again. We will never have another day exactly like today, so let's take advantage of the lessons we're offered.

We don't like to make mistakes, and we don't
like to be in situations that are fraught with stress,
but mistakes and distress seem to go along with
being human and alive. Both can be turned into
sound learning experiences.

We don't learn if we try to deny or ignore the
situation we don't like or don't handle well; nor
do we learn if we try to fix unpleasant circumstance with over- and undereating. How much
better if we can accept the difficulty, see how we
have contributed to it, and arrive at a positive
course of action. And how often it helps to talk
about the problem with someone else instead of
pridefully insisting on muddling through alone.
Very likely, we will discover that today's richest
learning experiences are those we share with
others.

---

*I will accept the lessons today offers and share
them with someone else so that we both can grow.*

We are the lucky ones.

We have found a way out of the misery of abusing food and our bodies. Today, we don't have to overeat, undereat, binge, purge, or be obsessed with diets and calories. There is a whole new world waiting for us to explore. We feel good about ourselves without depending on the numbers registered on a scale. We enjoy what we eat, but food is no longer the focal point of our existence. We have found a Higher Power.

How do we share our good fortune? We can help others find their way to recovery by telling them what has worked for us — if they ask. We can participate in existing support groups and start new ones.

We are fortunate indeed, but we know how dangerous it is for us to become complacent. We remember that we are always one bite away from a binge and that sharing our recovery enables us to maintain it.

Reminding ourselves how lucky we are keeps us grateful — grateful to the people who have helped us and to the Higher Power that helps us all.

Wherever I am in my recovery today, I am grateful to be finding answers to share.

*We didn't write the script, but we
can play our part.*

The drama of our life unfolds as we live it. Since we're not the playwright, we don't know what the next scene will bring, but we can keep body, heart, mind, and spirit in the best possible shape for whatever action is to occur.

We take our cues from those around us, and we believe that a Higher Power is in charge. The Twelve Steps are gently releasing us from the tyranny of feeling we must always be on center stage. Fortunately, that's not necessary or possible. Our role is important, but we are only one in a cast of billions.

Finding our place, moving gracefully and appropriately, learning our lines so we spontaneously respond to the opportunity of the moment, blending harmoniously with our fellow players — this is the art of a lifetime. This is what recovery is all about.

May I play my part in the action planned for today.

*The stamp of self-approval goes
along with recovery.*

As we recover from an eating disorder, we can also recover from being our own harshest critic and become instead our staunchest supporter. Rather than looking for what we do wrong and downgrading our capabilities, we can appreciate the progress we have made and cheer ourselves on to continued success.

The Steps lead us to a new measure of success: inner peace and serenity. We know better than anyone where we have come from, our assets and our liabilities, and what it takes for us to be proud of our behavior. We are learning to heed the inner voice that directs our actions. When we have done the best we can with what we have where we are, we can be at peace, leaving outcomes to a Higher Power.

A mark of progress in the program is a growing sense of self-approval that does not depend on pleasing other people but comes from within, from knowing and appreciating that we are worthy children of the universe.

Today, I will support my efforts and my progress.

*Habits can work for us rather than
against us.*

The way we eat becomes a habit. We tend to
choose the same types of foods and eat them at
more or less the same time of day. Many of us got
into the habit of consuming large quantities of
high-carbohydrate, high-fat foods in the evening.
Some of us restricted our intake to a salad once a
day. Neither extreme served us well.

When we commit ourselves to a healthy food
plan and get outside help so that we stick with it,
we are setting up new habits, the kind that work
for us instead of against us. Each meal and each
day we follow our plan, we are reinforcing these
new habits.

Over time, recovery becomes a habit. We learn
to automatically select what makes us feel good.
We reject the substances, thoughts, and actions
that brought us pain and unhappiness. As our eating habits change, so do our feelings and attitudes.
Hope replaces despair. We know we can get well,
and we're willing to do what's necessary to make
progress.

*I want what I eat today, and how much, to rein-
force the habit of recovery.*

Recovery can benefit the entire family.

As we change, we function differently in our relationships with family members, and this in turn prompts them to behave differently toward us. Just as an eating disorder affects the entire family, so does recovery.

We are often reluctant to reveal our problem with food. In fact, family members usually know about it before we tell them, and when we do talk, they often react with more understanding than we had expected. An eating disorder provides no more reason for placing blame or being defensive than any other illness. Dealing with the problem is an opportunity for all members of the family to learn how to function better.

Getting our families involved in our recovery can be a positive experience for all concerned. With improved communication, everyone benefits. We can learn to be open and honest with those we love, ask for their help and support, and use the Steps and our insights to strengthen our family relationships.

I will have the courage today to be open and honest with my family so that they may participate in my recovery.

*When all else fails, follow the
directions.*

Experience demonstrates that the Twelve Step
program works. It works for people who are addicted to alcohol, other drugs, compulsive gambling, and other compulsive behaviors. It also
works for those of us who are addicted to food,
diets, or both.

The program works when we follow the directions. If we get stuck, we need to ask ourselves if
we are thoroughly doing our part: Have we taken
a Fourth Step inventory and shared it? Have we
made amends to the best of our ability? How
about prayer and meditation? Are we going to
meetings regularly and making phone calls? Do
we have a food plan and a sponsor? Are we focused on knowing and doing the will of a Higher
Power?

Ours is a simple program, but it's not easy.
Recovery requires our serious attention and commitment. We have tried other ways, the so-called
softer and easier ones, but they haven't worked
Now we have the directions for recovery. Let's
follow them.

*Because I am in recovery, I will not be too proud
or too smart today to follow the directions.*

When we fill our minds and hearts
with good thoughts and feelings,
there isn't room for discouragement.

We decide what thoughts we will entertain and what feelings we will cultivate. Right at this moment, I can let myself become preoccupied with an old grudge, or I can think about good things — the sun is shining, my basic needs are taken care of, and I have a friend to call.

Formerly, I used food in an attempt to alter my mood. That doesn't work for me anymore, if it ever did, and I now have better ways of dealing with discouragement and all the other negative thoughts and feelings that threaten my serenity.

It may well be that action is required for me to move out of the rut of discouragement. I may need to exercise, clean a closet, or talk to a friend so I can shift back into a positive mood. Filling my mind and heart may involve physical movement as well as mental and emotional conditioning.

Today lies before me. I can partake of its many delights and blessings. My plate will be full.

*Some short-term pleasures can bring
long-term pain.*

How well many of us know the long-term pain
that follows the fleeting "pleasure" of a binge or
of undereating! With abstinence, we pass up the
so-called pleasure of overeating or restricting in
favor of the far more lasting satisfaction of eating
moderate meals that promote good health and
emotional well-being.

Are there other areas of our lives where we
need to make similar choices? Some of us tend to
make impulsive purchases, spending beyond our
means and putting ourselves in long-term financial difficulty for a temporary thrill. Others of us
go off on emotional binges such as love affairs or
temper tantrums. When the love affair ends, the
result is pain for ourselves and others. Temper
tantrums also produce pain for everyone involved.

Fortunately, we can use the Steps to lead us
away from dangerous impulsiveness into a more
sane and balanced way of living. We are learning
to pass up the short-term thrill, to wait and work
for what will give us lasting satisfaction.

Today, may I act in my long-term best interest.

Sometimes the best we can do is wait.

When we're undecided about a course of action, forcing the issue one way or the other may not be wise. Even though we'd like to have the matter settled, keeping our options open might be the best approach. Waiting can be extremely difficult — we feel frustrated about not making a move — but waiting may be exactly what we need to do.

Remember, we are learning to cooperate with the flow of life, not straining to push it along or move it in a different direction. Our course of action will eventually become clear, but we have turned the timetable over to a Higher Power. One of our goals is to develop the patience to wait until we feel clear inner guidance about how to proceed.

Recovery tempers our impulsive tendencies. When we're convinced we are cared for by the Power that runs the universe, we don't need to push ourselves into hasty decisions. We can admit we don't know the answer. We can wait, believing that in our Higher Power's time we will discover which move to make.

May I have the patience to wait for clear directions.

Loving fills the empty space.

We tried to fill our emptiness with food, with compulsive exercise, with complicated rituals that masked starvation. We thought we would be satisfied and complete if our bodies looked like those of models in fashion magazines.

No matter how much food we consumed, the empty space was still there. No matter how much we starved ourselves, we still felt incomplete and unsatisfied. No amount of food, exercise, or dieting was enough to fill our inner emptiness.

In recovery, we are learning to reach out to other people and to a Higher Power for the nourishment our hearts and spirits crave. We are learning to ask, to receive, to give, to love. The more love we give away, the more love comes back to us, and the more completely our inner space is filled.

Today, I will look for opportunities to be loving

*What makes us think the next bite —
or a smaller clothes' size — will be
better?*

When our eating disorder was active, many of us thought satisfaction was just over the horizon. We thought we would find it in the next bite, a smaller clothes' size, another relationship, or a new job.

Chronic dissatisfaction, like other habits, can be replaced with a healthier one. We know now that more is not necessarily better. If we don't enjoy this bite, it's unlikely we'll enjoy the next one. If we can't accept ourselves as a size six, we probably won't as a size four either. If we eat more or less than our bodies need, we limit our ability to enjoy all the other gifts life offers us. If we aren't willing to work on the relationships we have, looking for new ones may not be the answer to our loneliness.

We should not avoid making changes when a job, a relationship, or a location is not right for us. But neither should we get caught in the illusion that more or different is necessarily going to be better. What we have now is what is real. Let's make the most of it.

Before I look around for more today, I will concentrate on appreciating and enjoying what I already have.

Life is a gift.

There may be parts of life we'd just as soon not have. But whether we realize it or not, our life is a gift. Making the most of this life we've been given means keeping ourselves in the best possible condition — physically, emotionally, and spiritually.

To do this, we need the right amounts of nourishing food, not too much and not too little. We need exercise, we need work, we need satisfying relationships, we need play, and we need a spiritual base.

Many needs go along with the gift of life. We could list them indefinitely. Looking ahead, we may wonder how they will all be met. We may worry. We may be afraid.

We are reassured by the belief that the same Higher Power that gives us life gives us the answers to our many needs, one day at a time.

I will have faith that along with the gift of life, I will also be given what I need to live it fully today.

Hope is what keeps us afloat.

Some days, nothing seems to go the way it should, or at least not the way we think it should! We may feel as though we are down at the bottom of a well, with no chance of rising to the surface in the near future.

For those of us who are compulsive overeaters, feelings of hopelessness can trigger thoughts of food and binges. Those of us who undereat are prompted by depression to further restrict our intake.

Now that we have a program and a support group, the days when nothing seems to go right do not need to spell disaster. We have Steps and tools with which to handle crises and hard times. Best of all, we are coming to believe that in spite of difficult days, there is a basic goodness and purpose to all of life. We have hope that out of the hard times will come growth and strength.

I will share my hope today with someone else so that it will become stronger.

August

*Sometimes we have to hurt to get
better.*

A certain amount of physical and perhaps emotional discomfort usually goes along with having a tooth fixed, but the result is positive. If we didn't have the treatment, eventually we would be in even greater discomfort. Recovery from an eating disorder is also likely to involve some pain, but the alternative — allowing the illness to progress — is worse.

Some of us may experience physical discomfort when we stop bingeing, purging, abusing laxatives, et cetera, because we will be going through withdrawal from a biochemical process to which we have become accustomed. All of us will probably experience emotional discomfort, since we have been using either too much or too little food to anesthetize our feelings. Those painful emotions that we have tried to cover up need to be experienced so that we can move through them and get on with our lives.

Yes, recovery will involve some pain for most of us, but by being willing to feel the pain we are able to be healed.

*Being willing to feel the hurts of today is part of
my recovery.*

• AUGUST 2 •

*What will be the brightest part of
today for you?*

Recovery opens a new world for us. Each day
we can look forward to so much more than meals,
binges, calories, and scales. We can discover a
host of activities and experiences, unrelated to
food, that bring us pleasure. The more open we
are to our surroundings, the more spontaneous
and unexpected these pleasures will be.

Perhaps today I will take in the full beauty of
flowers I never really noticed before. Maybe a
conversation with an old friend will carry both of
us to a deeper level of intimate sharing. It could
happen that, being more closely in touch with my
body, I will delight in a period of satisfying movement and exercise. Maybe I will find myself completely absorbed in a challenging project.

Taking note of our special moments each day,
perhaps recording them in a journal, provides
valuable information about who we are and who
we are becoming.

---

*I will pay close attention to today's special mo-
ments and learn from them.*

*Our hungers lead us to what will
satisfy.*

Hunger serves us well. Physical hunger
prompts us to eat the food we need to promote
and maintain health. Emotional hunger sends us
in search of companionship, intimacy, love. Our
hunger for achievement fuels our contribution to
the work of the world. And our spiritual hunger
leads us to a Power greater than ourselves. Peace,
unity, goodwill — all of these and more, we hunger for.

If we find ourselves trying to satisfy our hunger
in ways that don't work, it's time to reassess and
make changes. That's what we do when we come
to the Twelve Step program, admitting that our
false satisfactions have gotten out of hand and are
threatening destruction.

The satisfaction of our various hungers is
within reach. Much of what we crave we will find
within ourselves as we develop a relationship
with a Higher Power.

*I will explore my hunger today, so that it may
lead me to what satisfies.*

We can learn to relax.

Stress may have prompted us to keep our mouths busily chewing, and it undoubtedly played a role in our continual dieting and weigh-ins. Some of us were in a stressful contest to see how thin we could be, how much exercise we could do, or how perfect we could be.

As we learn to listen to the wisdom of the body, we begin to notice tension. We realize our jaw is clenched or our neck is stiff or we want to eat even though we just finished a meal. We need to take a deep breath and think about why we are straining and what it is that we are trying to achieve, repress, or overcome. We need to decide whether we can do whatever we are doing just as well if we don't clench our teeth.

Giving up our overachieving, unrealistic goals may be a prerequisite for relaxation. Being willing to slow down and not try to do six things at once may also be necessary. A conscious decision to practice being relaxed is something we can make many times a day, whenever we feel our serenity slipping. Take a deep breath. Take several. Slow down. Enjoy the quiet.

I will practice relaxing today, so that in time it will become a habit.

*Out of suffering come strength and
compassion.*

Until we have experienced grief and despair,
we do not fully fathom the depths of our inner
resources, nor can we lovingly empathize with
another's pain. Compassion, perhaps our greatest
and most human quality, is hammered out of the
raw material of suffering.

As recovery eases our pain and frees us to love,
we come to want to help others who are in trouble. Our increasing strength gives us the ability to
offer understanding and support to those we realize are also struggling. As we give, we receive; the
compassion we show to others heals us as well.

Suffering cracks our hard outer shell of self-
sufficiency and indifference, opening us to love
and concern. The compassion with which we respond can be as simple as a gesture or a touch on
the shoulder that says, I understand, and I'm on
your side.

*I will use today's suffering in a way that will
make me stronger and more compassionate.*

Our bodies are where we live.

At some point, did you declare war on your body, rejecting its size and shape and vowing to make it conform to what you saw in the magazines?

No matter how hard we try, we're not all going to look like models. An important aspect of recovery is becoming comfortable with the bodies we have.

Some of us are tall, some of us are short, some of our bodies come with a small-boned frame, others are stocky. We each have a set point at which our weight stabilizes according to our individual requirements. When we come to terms with our given physical characteristics, we stop threatening our health and happiness with unreasonable demands on our bodies. Then the body is no longer the enemy but a friend, a source of pleasure.

Recovery teaches us to respect and care for our bodies. We learn to move them joyfully and have fun with them. Making peace with the body sets us free to use it instead of abuse it. Our bodies will be with us as long as we live. They deserve the best.

I am grateful that through recovery, my body has become my friend.

Much of our anxiety is nameless and needless.

Do you know what it's like to have a chronic sense of dread, as though disaster is awaiting you? Some of us have tried to relieve our anxiety with too much food, and some of us have used restriction and eating rituals as if they were magic that could make the fear go away.

Where does the anxiety come from? We may have learned it from overprotective parents or other adults who gave us the impression that the world was filled with danger with which we would never be able to cope. We may create our own fears out of the unrealistic demands and distorted perceptions of self-will.

Avoiding anxiety or covering it up with food, diets, or compulsive exercise is not a solution. Rather, we need the courage to examine what scares us and confront our sense of dread. We will probably discover that much of our fear is self-centered and irrational. With the light we receive from a Higher Power and the Steps, our nameless fears and needless anxieties disappear like the shadows they are.

I remind myself today that, with help from my Higher Power, I can confront my fear.

To repair a broken relationship,
someone must make the first move.

I'm hurt, and so are you. I'm angry, and so are you. Perhaps we both have "just cause," but we will remain stalemated unless one of us is willing to begin making amends and moving toward reconciliation.

When a relationship with a friend, neighbor, co-worker, or family member is one of hostility, nobody wins. Both parties are uncomfortable. We know from experience that self-pity and anger are emotions we can't afford to let fester. They destroy serenity and send us in the direction of our eating disorder. We also know how hard it is to put aside our pride and make a move that will allow the other party to lower his or her defenses.

If I sincerely try to make amends, but my efforts are rejected — well, that's the risk I take. But if I don't take the risk, I will continue to be uncomfortable. The effort to make amends to the best of my ability helps me let go of festering hurt, anger, and resentment. Serenity returns.

May I not be too proud to do today what I can to make amends.

It's possible to cultivate the gift of awareness.

If we were fully aware of one-tenth of the sights, sounds, feelings, and sensations that make up our experience each day, we'd never be bored. What happens all too often is that we put blinders on our attention, becoming narrowly focused on only a very small percentage of what's going on around and within us.

Being rigidly self-willed limits our awareness. We can be so intent on specific procedures and outcomes that we miss the rich possibilities that lie outside our restricted range of concentration. Another way we reduce our awareness is by being afraid to experience what's uncomfortable.

When we cultivate an appreciation of the many facets of everyday events, when we let our feelings and reactions take place spontaneously, we have a wealth of material to keep us fully alive and interested.

Nonjudgmental awareness of what I see, hear, and feel today will provide me with rich experience.

*For a quick refresher, erase the
clutter from your mind.*

What we do when we meditate is clear our
minds of the busy thoughts that make us tired.
Turning over our worries and concerns, we can
operate without thinking for a time while we connect with the spiritual side of our lives.

Mental overload is uncomfortable. We know
what it is to stew ourselves into a state where we
try to relieve the pressure by bingeing, restricting,
or overexercising. That kind of relief is only temporary, and the after-effects can be disastrous.

Our minds are not meant to carry the weight of
the world, or even our own perplexities, non-
stop, without a breather. When we feel tension
and fatigue mounting, we can wipe our minds
clean for a few moments and give our spirits a
chance to recuperate. Sometimes it's good to forget, temporarily, everything we know, or think
we know. If we rest and let our consciousness be
blank for a time, we can then respond creatively
to the present, without being bound by preconceived ideas. It is in this way that insights come to
us and problems are solved.

*I will take time today to let my spirit refresh my
mind.*

How realistic is my body image?

Judging ourselves against unrealistic standards, many of us grew up thinking we were fat. Some of us may think of ourselves as fat, even though we have lost weight and are within a normal range for our height. Others of us may see ourselves as fat, even though other people consider us too thin. Still others of us may look at ourselves only from the neck up, ignoring what is below the neck because we don't like what we see.

Many of us have a distorted body image — this often goes along with an eating disorder. Some of us are persuaded by messages from the media that an exaggerated thinness is ideal. Others of us would like to think we're fine, when actually we're dangerously overweight. In each case, we distort or deny reality.

If I have doubts about my best weight, I can check with a doctor. If I am trying to conform to a standard that does not suit my body type, I need to reconsider. Developing a realistic image of our bodies as they are now and as they are at their healthiest is an important part of recovery.

Maybe it would be a good idea for me to check out the accuracy of my body image today with someone whose judgment I respect.

Hurts do heal.

Time has a wonderful way of erasing bad feelings and leaving us with good ones. Our memories are selective, and fortunately, the pleasant ones seem to have more staying power. Whatever has been real and meaningful for us tends to remain with us — the rest gradually fades away. We can assist this selective process of memory by consciously letting go of the thoughts and feelings that disturb our serenity.

You might imagine yourself making a package out of a disappointment, your hostility, some hurt feelings, or whatever is hampering your spirit. Wrap the package tightly and ship it off to a Higher Power. Send it air mail, if you like.

Refusing to dwell on our wounds allows them to heal more quickly. In our program, there is no place for self-pity. The reprieve we have from our eating disorder is a daily one, and it depends on our spiritual condition. Gratitude for all the good fortune that comes our way keeps us healthy.

I will remember that what hurts today will pass in time. I can speed its departure by refusing to indulge in self-pity.

*When we are willing and able to
give love, we shall receive it.*

If only I had the right relationship, my eating disorder would disappear. This is a thought that has crossed many of our minds. In the past, some of us have tried to make food a substitute for love, as well as a substitute for sex. Others of us have allowed the obsession with being thin to undermine our ability to have a satisfying relationship.

We need love. Food and diets won't substitute. And we need love from more than just one special person. The more loving we are able to be in all our contacts with others, the more nourishment comes back to feed our hearts and spirit.

By making a commitment to practice abstinence and the Twelve Steps, we put ourselves on the path of love. As our harmful compulsions are lifted, we have new energy to focus on our relationships with those whose lives we touch. We find a source of spiritual strength and insight that enables us to give love as well as receive it. Daily, we make ourselves ready.

I will practice love today.

Those we love deserve our undivided attention.

Being fully present in our interaction with another person is our contribution toward assuring that the encounter will have meaning for both of us. In the past, many of us have let our attention be distracted either by thoughts of the next binge or the after-effects of the last one. Others of us have been emotionally shut down and unavailable because of our obsession with dieting and exercising.

Perhaps we still permit distractions to interfere with our concentration when we are with someone we care about. Whether the person is a friend, lover, child, or other family member, he or she deserves our total awareness. Planning what we will do next or thinking about what happened earlier does not allow us to fully attend and respond to the person we love. The potential of the encounter is diluted.

Through recovery, our full power of concentration becomes available to us to share with others.

My gift of attention today will help nurture my relationships.

*The glow of inner satisfaction is
stronger and lasts longer than the
sound of external applause.*

Applause is great, and we all like to be appreciated for a job well done. Approval from others, however, is not always forthcoming, and it doesn't go as far toward sustaining our efforts as doing what satisfies us. When we do things to please someone else, the rewards can wear thin fairly rapidly. Besides, the other person may not be as pleased as we had expected or hoped.

How good it is to feel the satisfaction of knowing we have done our best in an undertaking that is important to us! Perhaps we didn't get any applause. Perhaps our efforts went largely unnoticed. But we knew and were pleased.

We don't have to win outside awards in order to feel inner satisfaction. Probably no one will give me a medal for following my food plan today, but I will be pleased with myself. And that's what counts in the long run.

Today, I will cultivate my own approval.

*We can be strong enough to risk
failure and rejection.*

If perfectionism and people-pleasing have been among our problems, then the possibility of failing or being rejected has probably filled us with dread. We may have avoided a challenge — learning to ski, for example — because we were afraid we would look foolish and not do well. Or, we might be holding back in our interpersonal relations, not making the first move because we fear the other person might not respond the way we would hope.

We will know we're on the road to recovery when we're willing to try something we want to do, and reach out to someone we care about, just because we want to, never mind the outcome. If the outcome is less than perfect, or if we get rejected, we will survive. And we can always try again or try something or someone else.

Recovery strengthens our self-esteem. We are finding solutions to problems that may have baffled us for a long time.

I won't be perfect today, and I may be rejected, but I'll have the satisfaction of acting on my inner motivation.

*The winds of adversity release our
spiritual resources.*

We've all probably had the experience of going beyond the limits of the strength we thought we had, of getting a second wind when we feared we were reaching the point of exhaustion. Looking back, we wonder how we ever got through a particularly difficult time. And yet, we not only survived it but were able to draw from a storehouse of reserve energy we didn't even know we possessed.

This shows that we don't know what we can do until we try. And, human nature being what it is, we're often not inclined to try unless we're challenged by stormy circumstance. The winds of trouble that threaten to uproot us are the very forces that break through "I can't" and "I won't."

Let's give thanks for the storms of life that shake us out of complacency and release our latent energy and capabilities. Let's be grateful for the difficult experiences that release our spiritual resources and point us to a source of strength beyond ourselves.

---

*Today's troubles can help me find energy
reserves I didn't know I had.*

Self-will is exhausting.

Many of us have worked ourselves into a frenzy over something that simply would not turn out according to our best-laid plans. We can get upset over anything from a piece of equipment that won't work properly to a relationship that appears to be drifting or on the rocks. In desperation, we may try to "fix" the problem with excess food or self-starvation.

Insisting on our will, our way, and our schedule is usually an extremely frustrating experience. It's like trying to push water uphill: we wear ourselves out. And we're subject to much fear, since deep down we have a sinking feeling that insisting on our way may not work.

What a relief it is to take Step Three and accept our Higher Power's will for our lives. This acceptance applies to the small details of each day as well as to the big picture. We do our part the best we can, but the outcome belongs to a Power greater than ourselves. Therein lies serenity.

Just for today, I will accept my Higher Power's will and be serene.

*Sometimes the question is not what
do we want but what can we give.*

Wanting more and more gets us into trouble.
How well we know that! It's not that our wanting
more and more doesn't reflect a need — it does.
But often what we need most is nonmaterial.
When we're dissatisfied, we may think we need
something more to eat, new clothes to wear, or
another piece of sports equipment. And, perhaps
we do. But then again, perhaps these new acquisi-
tions will leave us feeling unsatisfied still.

It's possible that what we really need is the satisfaction that comes from giving rather than taking.
When we give love, our hearts are no longer
empty. When we give time and energy to a useful
project, we gain a feeling of inner satisfaction.
When we contribute a service to someone else,
we feel valuable and needed.

The more we give, freely and because we
choose to, the stronger our self-esteem becomes
and the less we turn to food and compulsive activity to fill an inner emptiness.

What will I give today?

*We won't know if a decision will
work until we put it into action.*

Reasons for — reasons against. Sometimes we
are pulled in both directions, with our head going
one way and our heart another. We are often
afraid that we will regret a course of action that
nevertheless appears to be the way to go.

Our big decisions are rarely made without
backward glances and tugs toward the road not
taken. That's because, often, in order to go after
something we want, we must let go of something
we already have. We wonder if the new route will
really be better or if we will be sorry we took it.

Once we plant our feet firmly on the chosen
road and support our choice with actions, the forward momentum carries us along, and we begin
to feel more sure. It's at the crossroad that we hesi-
tate. That's where we listen hard for the inner
voice of direction, which may very well be
prompting us to do what initially seems more difficult but which will move us toward our ultimate
goal.

*The proof of my decisions today will be in my
actions.*

We need time and space, as well as movement.

The world of recovery is an active one, and we are grateful that we can participate fully. We are doing things we never before had the energy, confidence, or motivation to accomplish.

And we're more than ever aware of the need for moderation, in activity as well as in our food plan. Those of us who are recovering from an eating disorder can all too easily run and do and be busy to the point of exhaustion, even when we're having fun! Is it worth it? Not if our hard-won serenity is swept away in the flurry of activity.

The tools of the program serve us well in structuring our daily schedule along with our food plan. Time for rest, space to be alone, opportunities to connect with our spiritual center — these belong in each day so that we don't get lost in movement and activity.

May the quiet moments and spaces of today nurture my activity.

*Comparing ourselves with others is
often counterproductive.*

Each of us is unique. When we start comparing
ourselves with someone else, we are asking for
trouble. We see the outside of the other person,
which may seem considerably stronger, better, or
luckier than the way we feel ourselves to be. So
we injure our self-esteem. We feel inadequate, as
though we don't measure up.

What counts is what we do with what we have.
Our Higher Power expects us to be and do the
best we can, but does not expect us to be someone else or to do what that person does. We don't
want to be so focused on trying to emulate another person that we lose sight of our unique gifts
and our individuality.

Your path is not my path. My job is to find out
what I need and what I can contribute. My body
type may be different than yours, as may my food
plan, choice of friends, and career objectives. The
beauty of recovery is that we learn how to be ourselves. We allow ourselves to develop our special
talents, to honor our likes and dislikes, to choose
the path we will follow.

*If I am comparing myself with someone else to-
day, I will remember that I'm meant to be myself.*

I came to believe that I would have enough.

For some of us, our eating disorders were related to a fear of material insecurity. Our binges may have been, at times, ways of compensating for things we did not have and, also, attempts to relieve anxiety about what we thought we would lack in the future.

The fear that we did not or would not have enough was an irrational anxiety that required spiritual attention. It could only be banished by gratitude and by faith and trust in a Power greater than ourselves. Experience has proved that the more we rely on this Power, the richer our lives become — in every way.

When we tap into our spiritual resources, we open ourselves to a reservoir of abundance. We find what we need, and much more. There is, however, a condition that is placed on our enjoyment of the abundance — we must share our wealth. This brings us to the Twelfth Step, carrying the message and practicing the principles.

My material supplies are more than enough when I use my spiritual resources.

The longer we choose what's good
for us, the better we like it.

When our taste buds are not distorted by quantities of refined sugar and junk food, we can savor and appreciate the flavor of wholesome, natural fruits, vegetables, and grains. When we stop trying to achieve an artificial high through restricting and exercising compulsively, our spirits rise to natural and comfortable levels of buoyancy.

If we stay with abstinence long enough — abstinence from what harms our body and depresses our spirit — we come to realize that we are not really giving up anything of value. Instead, we are gaining health and well-being. We are finding new energy and vitality.

If ever we're tempted to go back to old habits, we can remember the misery that accompanied them. We have been given a way out of that misery, and we want to leave it behind us forever. Each day that we choose what's good for us, we strengthen our recovery.

Today, I choose recovery.

We are part of a powerful network.

Following a Twelve Step program makes us part of the recovering community. Whether we have been addicted to food, diets, alcohol, drugs, gambling, sex, or a combination, the Steps are a bond that links us together in the exciting adventure of a new way of life. We are convinced that happiness and satisfaction are not to be found in substances and compulsive behavior, and we are exploring alternatives.

The adventure leads us into the realm of the spiritual. It is there that we find what does satisfy our craving. We give each other the freedom to choose how we will develop the spiritual component in our lives, and we offer support to all who wish to join us.

Though we have different ways of defining a Higher Power, we come to believe in a spiritual reality that makes a difference in our lives and that makes possible our recovery. We use the power of the group, our support network, to enrich our lives and to keep us on track.

I will reach out today to give and receive support in the Twelve Step program.

When we let go of surface thoughts,
we can hear our inner voice.

Our thoughts chase each other around the outside of our awareness until we are worn out: We have to do this, remember that, figure out something else. We feel stress, tension, excitement, frustration. We need to relax, but not with excess food, extreme exercise, or self-starvation.

We want answers to our pressing life questions. We want to know which course of action we should take, how to handle a difficult situation.

We have an ever-present source of peace, an inner guide that points us in the right direction and tells us what we need to know. We gain access to it by letting go of our busy surface thoughts and listening to the calm voice that speaks deep within the center of our being.

―――――――――――――

Right now I will let my noisy outer thoughts subside, and I will listen to my inner voice.

Abstinence is a foundation for intimacy.

Isolation accompanies eating disorders. If we overeat, we are trying to use food to fill emotional needs, and the result is often a wall of fat that "protects" us from others. If we binge and purge or starve ourselves, our energy is drained by the compulsive behavior. We are not as emotionally available to others as we should be.

At one time, we may have thought food was the best friend we had, but it let us down. So did dieting. Now that we are recovering, we can use more of our energy to connect with the people around us, our families and friends. When we stop hiding in bingeing, purging, or compulsive dieting, we can begin to learn to trust other people to satisfy our needs for love and belonging.

Intimacy rewards us with the deep sharing and acceptance we crave. Abstinence makes this reward possible.

My abstinence can support me as I reach out today to someone close to me.

*Turning liabilities into assets is
what our program is about.*

Out of weakness — strength. Because I could not cope with my eating disorder on my own, and because my life had become unmanageable, I had to get help. I tried various types of Band-Aids, which didn't work, and then I found the Twelve Step program. It works.

We come to the program because of our problems with food, and we find help for our living problems as well. By admitting our weaknesses, we are able to be open to a Power greater than ourselves, a Power that can turn our lives around.

Was I out of control? Yes. Was I angry, fearful, resentful, depressed, arrogant? Yes. The program shows me how to exchange these liabilities for discipline, serenity, confidence, hope, humility, forgiveness, faith — the list expands as I go deeper into recovery.

I am grateful for the strength of the program.

*We can give ourselves permission to
feel our feelings.*

Years of conditioning may have put us in a position of denying and repressing our feelings, particularly those that evoke distress — our distress or someone else's. We have perhaps been afraid that acknowledging and expressing those feelings would bring down some kind of disaster, or that we might be overwhelmed by their intensity.

When we struggle to deny or repress emotions, we fight ourselves and remain off balance. We're unable to resolve the issues.

The next time I experience a wave of anger, embarrassment, fear, or sadness, or the next time I'm upset but don't know why, I can stop whatever I'm doing and allow myself to feel my feelings. I can go with them and say, "Yes, I'm angry, sad, _____, and this is how it feels." I may find that I've reclaimed a part of myself.

*Whatever I feel today is part of my wholeness. I
will not be afraid to experience it fully.*

Hope is best kept alive by sharing it.

Hope blossoms inside us when we hear how others are recovering from their problems with food and from the unmanageability of their lives. When we hear these people's stories in their own words, we know it can be done and that we can do it too. The Twelve Steps knit us together into a recovering community. Through the experience, strength, and hope we share with each other, we can find solutions to our common problems.

Staying in touch, going to meetings, using the telephone — these are ways we strengthen our recovery. We need to remind each other that life after abstinence is infinitely better than our old addictive patterns of behavior. By supporting each other and by being available to listen and share, we reinforce our determination to continue making progress.

Hope is what we found when out of despair we reached for help. We keep that hope alive and well by giving it away.

I will share my hope today.

*When we are comfortable being
alone, we are able to love another
person.*

If I use other people to try to escape myself, I
encounter many of the same problems I'd tried to
solve with my unhealthy eating habits. When I am
able to be alone comfortably, I can enter a relationship with another person — a relationship we
both choose and one that produces mutual fulfillment, not clinging dependency.

The self-knowledge and confidence we gain
from spending time alone make it unnecessary to
crave confirmation of our worth from an outside
source. When we have that, we are able to love
other people as they are, rather than for what we
want them to do for us.

Another person cannot give me myself or provide me with self-esteem. When I am not afraid to
be alone, when I enjoy my own company, when
my self-esteem is strong — then I can love someone else without losing myself.

*I will cultivate my ability to love someone else by
enjoying my time alone today.*

September

Even times of joy can be stressful.

Celebrations can be dangerous for those of us who have problems with food. We may be tempted to deviate from our food plan, which makes us vulnerable to a binge. Or we may get so excited and high on the good times that we neglect to get the nourishment we need.

As we become more secure in ourselves and with our Higher Power, we are less overcome by emotional highs and lows. Even when we are very, very happy we know we need to continue the daily routine we have established for our recovery. The conviction that a power greater than ourselves is in charge can protect us from an emotional overload of good feelings as well as bad ones.

When we do not dull our feelings by either too much or too little food, we need a new source of stability so that we are not overwhelmed by powerful emotions. That source of stability is ever-present as we learn to center ourselves in the peace and serenity that come from trusting our Higher Power to give us what we need each day.

I am learning how to handle the stress of joy as well as sorrow.

Our mistakes teach us what not to do.

One of the benefits of humility is that we more readily learn from our mistakes. Instead of berating ourselves for not being perfect, we can accept the fact that, yes, we frequently make errors. We do our best to correct the damage, and then we move on, wiser than before.

It is when we deny having taken a turn in the wrong direction that we are likely to get thoroughly lost and off course. Realizing we are on the wrong pathway and being willing to ask for directions helps us make the necessary correction.

If we are so afraid of making a mistake that we avoid taking risks and exploring new possibilities, we limit our opportunities for growth. Sometimes we need to try a course of action before we can know whether it will work for us. If it doesn't, we don't have to try it again.

I will look at today's mistakes as learning experiences.

Try cruising above the turbulence.

We all have these times: We're tired. We have a million things to do. Members of our family are fighting. There is a crisis at work. Our thoughts are churning.

Picture what it's like to be on an airplane as it climbs higher, gaining altitude to rise above a storm. Bounced by air turbulence, it cuts through the clouds, and then it emerges into the blue sky. The sun returns (it was always there — just obscured by the clouds), and the ride becomes so smooth that there is hardly any sensation of motion.

In a similar way, we can rise above stormy events and our own inner turbulence. We can cruise at a different altitude. To reach that new level of tranquility, we can use various methods from relaxation techniques to meditation to the Serenity Prayer to taking a walk or a shower or a nap.

———————————

Since a Higher Power is in control of my life, I can cruise above the turbulence.

*One cure for feeling crummy is to do
something for someone else.*

When we're feeling low, there's a high that
won't harm our bodies, minds, or spirits. In fact,
it's good for us. This is the high that comes from
being of service, helping, doing something useful
for another person. When we turn our attention
to another human being and make an effort to
raise his or her spirits, we too feel better. The understanding and encouragement we give away
comes back to us.

We've tried other ways of feeling better — eating food we did not need, getting thinner than
was healthy, overexercising. These ways were
lonely, and we ended up feeling worse.

Of course, if we are severely depressed, we
need to get professional help. For garden-variety
blues and blahs, however, each day offers relief in
the form of opportunities to reach out and share.
If we try concentrating on making someone else
feel good, we may be pleasantly surprised at what
happens to us.

*I can do something for another person today that
will make us both feel better.*

When we really want to do something, we find the time.

This day holds twenty-four hours for each of us. That's time enough to do a great many things but not everything. We must pick and choose and set priorities.

When recovery is our number-one priority, we find the time to do what's needed to keep getting better. We make time in our busy schedules for meetings, talking to sponsors and friends, making food plans, buying and preparing the food we need, reading recovery-oriented literature.

If we really want to get to know ourselves more completely, develop our potential more fully, and cultivate a more satisfying relationship with a Higher Power, we will take time to sit still and listen to our inner voice. We will let the insights we gain direct our daily activities. By doing this, we invest our energy where it brings the highest return for ourselves and others.

I want recovery and spiritual growth to be my priorities today.

Why not think about what's right instead of what's wrong?

On any given day, if we try, most of us can easily think of at least twenty-five things that are wrong with our lives, and probably about two hundred fifty that are wrong with the world in general. These lists are generated, presumably free of charge, by our negative perspective. There are, however, some horrendous hidden costs. When our attitude is constantly one of criticism, when we go around looking for what's wrong wherever we are, we are courting depression and discouragement, setting ourselves up to attract negative responses.

On the other hand, we can view the same day and the same situations from a different perspective, a positive one. We can look for what's right with ourselves, our lives, and the wider universe of which we're all a part.

It shouldn't be difficult to come up with twenty-five good things in our life today, and at least two hundred fifty in the world at large. It's worth trying, just to remind ourselves that we deserve to feel good.

For today, I will catalog what's right.

I am more than my weight.

Whether I am size extra small, small, medium, large, or extra large, my poundage is only one aspect of the total me. We are each a child of creation. Every one of us is special. We each have an important contribution to make.

We have the opportunity to discover our potential, the totality of our being, which transcends size and weight. We can accept ourselves just as we are, at this moment, whether we are thin or fat or in the middle, because the body we have right now is the one in which our complete self lives.

Nurturing that self is what we are doing when we follow the Twelve Steps along with our food plan. We are unlocking our potential as complete human beings, as we work in recovery to develop our spiritual, emotional, and physical sides. A Higher Power directs the unfolding of our total personality.

I can be assured of my individual worth and dignity, whatever I weigh today.

*The way to overcome being afraid is
to do what we fear.*

We get over a fear of heights by gently exposing ourselves to high places, raising the level of elevation a bit at a time. Having a friend with us helps, but even when we're alone, we can count on the support of a Higher Power. We don't need to fear crowded places, open spaces, speaking in public, or flying in an airplane. Gradual exposure, combined with techniques of relaxation, can help us reduce our fearful reactions. If necessary we can get professional help.

When we don't challenge ourselves to overcome our fears, our lives tend to become more and more constricted as we find elaborate ways of avoiding situations that create anxiety. Our eating disorders feed our fears, and vice versa.

The recovery experience assures us that change is possible. We can get over the fears that prevent us from realizing our potential and enjoying each day. Let's seek the courage to change the things we can, to ask for the help we need, and to be patient with ourselves as we unlearn our fearful responses.

Can I do one thing today that I was afraid to do yesterday?

We can't hasten the dawn.

Dark hours. We all have them. We would like to make them pass quickly so that we will once again be back in the light. Sometimes we wonder if the light will ever return. The dark hours before dawn can seem very long indeed.

We can learn to accept both light and dark, joy and sorrow, as complimentary components of the whole that is our life experience. With patience and courage, we can go through the dark times, securely trusting in ultimate goodness.

We can't speed the dawn, but we can remember and cherish the light that comes to us in our moments of meditation, in our sharing with loved ones, in beauty that we see and hear and feel. We can have faith that the dark hours, too, are part of our progress, that the promises of the program are at work within us, and that out of the darkness will come new growth and light.

I will be secure in the knowledge that day follows night, even if dawn comes more slowly than I would like.

*We don't have to be good
at everything.*

An overachieving "super person" is hard to live with, especially when that person is me. A dash of humility brings welcome relief from the pressure of thinking that we should excel at whatever we do.

We can become more realistic in our expectations of ourselves. One way to do this is to make choices about where we will concentrate our energies. We can determine what means most to us, do our very best in those areas, and let go of less rewarding activities and projects.

I may never swim the English Channel or win any housekeeping awards, nor am I likely to be Ms. America, but that's okay. As I trust in my Higher Power, I can better use the talents and abilities I have and learn to be more tolerant of my deficiencies. Recovery includes being able to choose where I will focus my energies and not expecting perfection.

Today, I will be selective in what I do and tolerant of my imperfections.

*Fear of pain can be more uncom-
fortable than pain itself.*

Whether it's a visit to the dentist, a confrontation with the boss, or having to tell a loved one
something she or he would prefer not to hear, we
may contemplate the experience with dread. We
fear someone will be hurt, either ourselves or a
person important or dear to us.

The anticipation of pain that we build up in our
mind can cause more distress and last longer than
the actual hurt. Doesn't it make more sense to stay
with the present moment, leaving possible future
pain to be dealt with when and if it happens? That
way, we have to endure only the actual discomfort, which may turn out to be far less intense that
we imagined. We are expected only to handle
reality, moment by moment.

And when we stay with the reality of the moment, we have immediate support. Our Higher
Power gives us the strength and courage we need
for the present time. We can let go of our fear of
future pain, accepting only what hurts right now.

*The pain of this present moment is all I need to
endure.*

*If we never get turned down, we
may not be asking for enough.*

We probably won't get all that we want — from
our family, our friends, our job, life itself — but
we have the ability to ask. It's certain that if we're
afraid to ask because the answer may be no, we reduce our chances of having a promotion, a date,
or help with the dishes.

Some of us vacillated between the extremes of
demanding more than our share, and feeling that
all we really deserved were leftovers. Food and
eating became an arena where our unresolved
needs and wants were acted out.

Knowing what we want and how much we
need are lessons of recovery. We learn them in the
kitchen, bedroom, shopping mall, office, at
school, and on the playing field — wherever we
are. We don't learn them all at once, nor do we
learn them without being willing to make requests. We can risk being turned down because
we believe that, one way or another, we will receive what we need.

*Today, I will ask for three things I would like to
have.*

Looking back, we can see where we've been.

When we're in transit, growing psychologically, we're not always sure where we are. In fact, we may frequently be confused, wondering why we're experiencing unrest, apprehension, or uneasiness. We hack through the emotional underbrush, clearing the way so we can advance, but we may not know where the path leads. We may lose sight of familiar landmarks, but we press on, hoping we're moving forward.

Transitional periods in our recovery come when we make important changes: We give up the security of a familiar job for a new one with more potential and challenge. We move out of a relationship that is detrimental to our growth. We undergo a powerful experience that alters our philosophical outlook on life.

Going through a transitional stage is like climbing a hill. There comes a time when we reach the top, turn around and look behind at the terrain we've covered, and recognize the progress we've made. It's a good feeling.

If I'm not sure where I am today, I will take time to look back and appreciate the progress I've made.

Take time out to do nothing.

Some of us will do anything to avoid "wasting" time. So we clutter up the spaces of our lives with busywork and time fillers, and then we wonder why we feel harassed.

Growth and creativity require empty space. The time we spend "doing nothing" can give our minds and bodies a chance to relax and our spirit the opportunity to breathe freely and become recharged. The empty spaces in life don't need to be filled with compulsive activity any more than they need to be filled with food or diets. These spaces can become periods of tranquility when we sit still and contemplate a beautiful landscape, a gentle breeze, a warm feeling, or a new idea.

We're not really doing nothing during these quiet times. We're allowing our inner self to come forth. We're receiving spiritual nourishment, and we're giving ourselves time and space for new insights to occur.

The empty spaces of today will nourish my spirit.

Recovering takes practice.

No one learns how to play golf in a day, or masters a musical instrument in a week, or builds a relationship in a month. Neither does recovery happen overnight.

If we're ready and lucky, we may immediately take the direct path of abstinence and stay on it without making any detours. When that occurs, it's wonderful, but it's just a beginning. Recovering is more than abstaining from overeating, bingeing and purging, or restricting. Recovering is a new way of life that involves our entire being.

What, when, and how much we eat is the starting point. Then we move on to how we think, feel, act, and believe. Before we're very far along the path, we realize we're learning a whole new way of orienting ourselves to the events of every day. It feels good, and the more we practice, the more complete our recovery.

I give thanks for another day to practice recovering.

*With abstinence, we view the world
through sparkling clean windows.*

Too much food puts us in a fog; similarly, too little distorts our perception. Either way, we go through the motions of the day, but we're not fully present. We feel dull, and whatever we experience is also dulled.

With the right amount of healthy nourishment, all of our senses are sharpened. What previously appeared blurred takes on new clarity. It's as though we had been living in a house with dirty windows, looking at the view outside through cloudy glass, until one day we washed the windows, inside and out.

What a difference! Our perception clears, and what we see is sharply focused. The light sparkles, and colors are vivid. It's the same view, but the fog is gone.

So, too, with abstinence. The external circumstances of our lives may remain basically the same, but we are functioning with new clarity and focus. The fog has lifted; we are seeing clearly.

*I am thankful today for the sparkle abstinence
gives me.*

*Conversations from the heart feed
our spirit.*

A steady diet of superficial chitchat results in a malnourished soul and a sense of isolation. All of us hunger for meaningful, heart-to-heart communication. When we experience it, our spirits feel full.

Even a brief conversation with a stranger on a bus can be meaningful if we are speaking with honesty and sincerity and expressing important feelings, and if we are willing to lower our defenses and be ourselves. (And ironically, it's sometimes easier to be candid with a stranger on a bus than with a family member or close friend.)

Speaking from the heart leaves us vulnerable and exposed. We are revealing our tender emotions, and we fear the listener might use our vulnerability to his or her advantage. Yes, there's a risk, but if one of us is willing to take it, the other can follow suit. And then, satisfying communication can nourish us both.

Today, I will tell at least one person something that comes from my heart.

Daily our spirits are renewed.

For most of us, a spiritual awakening does not come once and for all. Instead, we have small flashes of insight here and there, and every once in a while we look back and realize with gratitude how the promises of the program have been coming true for us.

Just as our bodies need daily nourishment, so do our spirits. We can seek people and experiences that leave us feeling warm and uplifted. We can take time each day to become quiet in mind and body so that we hear the inner messages that refresh our spirits. We can read something inspirational, listen to good music, look at a beautiful painting or a sunset, grasp a friend's hand in understanding, say a prayer.

Our spirits bounce back from hurt and depression. They are more easily renewed when we take proper care of our bodies, since we are a total entity of heart, mind, body, and spirit.

Today, I will look for ways to feed my spirit.

To love one's work is to be blessed.

One of recovery's greatest gifts is the ability to choose where we will concentrate our efforts, to work hard at those tasks, and to love the feeling of accomplishing something useful. We are instruments of a Higher Power — life's instruments — and when we function effectively, we experience joy and satisfaction.

As we come to know ourselves better in recovery, we may discover we need to find a more fulfilling job. We may decide to invest our time and talents in what for us is a new venture. Some of us would describe our career trajectory since becoming abstinent as nothing short of miraculous, the kind of miracle that quietly occurs when we patiently cultivate the courage to change the things we can.

We can make no finer contribution to the work of the world than to love what we do and do it conscientiously. With abstinence, we multiply our effectiveness and our satisfaction, whatever it is we choose to do.

Today, I will work with love and abstinence.

*If we practice being open, we will
receive abundantly.*

Life beyond the food obsession is like breathing fresh air. We're no longer smothered in calories, diets, and binges, nor held hostage by the scales. We don't have to cling and grasp and protect. Letting go of obsessions and compulsions, we stand open and empty, ready to receive the gifts each day presents.

In Step One, we admit our need. Steps Two and Three introduce us to a source of abundance that can be ours when we tap our inner resources, the Higher Power of our understanding. The remaining nine Steps show us how we can reorganize our lives so we will be ready to receive the gifts that are ours.

Being humble, teachable, willing to try new ways, and asking for help, are all keys to recovery. The price is letting go of self-will, so we can be open and responsive to a Power greater than ourselves.

Each day is a fresh page. If we don't fill it up with yesterday's regrets and tomorrow's worries, we will have room for the abundant and unexpected blessings of today.

I will be open today to the gifts of the present.

*You can feel only your own feelings,
not another person's.*

Having empathy for those we love, and being able to share their joys and sorrows, is part of our nature as warm, caring human beings. Taken to an extreme, however, too much empathy can mean that we lose our boundaries as emotionally separate individuals. When that happens, nobody wins.

We're responsible for our own feelings. If we're too deeply involved in another person's emotional state, we may not be truly aware of our own feelings. If we take on someone else's response to a situation, we lose our own in the process.

In any situation, particularly one that is highly charged with negative emotions, we need to maintain a sense of self. If we allow ourselves to be swept up in the anger, fear, grief, or despair of someone close to us, we become less capable of giving help and support. Emotional maturity is one of the goals of recovery. We progress toward it as we differentiate how we feel from how another person appears to feel.

I can respect the feelings of others without making them my own.

We can be calm in the midst of crisis.

Every once in a while we experience major up-heavals in our lives, and more often we go through minor dislocations. Sometimes we deal with the major crises better than with the minor ones. The big problems may challenge us to respond by drawing on our inner reserves, while the little ones often seem to be unnecessary annoyances.

Whatever the magnitude of the crisis we face, our program helps us maintain equanimity and balance. We do not need to be thrown off recovery's course by big or little disruptions in our daily routines. We can tap a source of strength beyond ourselves.

Starting with the Serenity Prayer, we can create a reservoir of calm as we follow Step Eleven into a daily practice of prayer and meditation. This reservoir will remain with us throughout the day and will supply us with the strength and peace we need when trouble comes.

I will fill and maintain my reservoir of calm today.

Accept no substitutes.

If something important seems to be missing in our lives, it's vital to keep asking until we know what it is. We first must identify what it is we're really lacking and then take concrete action to remedy the deficiency. Not every need or desire is easy to fill. But if we know what we want and are willing to work and wait for it, we can avoid the trap of getting hooked on substitutes for the real thing.

It's certain that we can't always have what we want when we want it. We can hope for the future, but what do we do in the meantime? Fantasizing about the perfect relationship while bingeing on butter cookies or starving on one salad a day does not bring the relationship any closer; on the contrary, real satisfaction is pushed further away.

We know there must be something to ease the pain of loneliness, calm our anxiety, and help us feel energetic instead of depressed. There is. By tuning in to our spiritual center, which is close at hand and always available, we find the strength and peace that helps us to work and wait for what we really want.

May I remember today that substitutes do not satisfy.

Humility invites learning.

An attitude of humility does not imply any lack of self-esteem, but it does mean we are open to learning from our experiences. If we think we know everything there is to know, we close down our faculty for absorbing new knowledge. We become calcified in a rut of habit and assumption. Humility is what softens our resistance to new ideas and procedures.

Humility allows us to admit we don't know all the answers, not even all the questions. Humility permits us to ask for help. When we're humble, we can take a wrong turn and not get lost, because we're willing to go back for additional directions.

The more we learn, the more we are aware of the wider world that remains to be explored. The Steps have launched us on a learning experience that takes us into the realm of spiritual growth. There, our options are limitless, and it is by staying humble that we are able to take advantage of them.

Being humble can open new doors for me today

Grace lifts us over the hurdles.

Some of us may be facing a huge ordeal, and we don't see how in the world we'll ever manage to survive it. Before abstinence, our first thought might have been to either binge or starve our way through it, but now we know those methods only make the hurdles higher and more difficult to clear.

There is another way. Knowing we are best equipped to meet a difficult challenge when we do not regress into our food obsession, we can keep abstinence as our number one priority. Then we can make a plan for handling the tough situation. We can decide how we need to prepare ourselves, where we can get help, who will give us advice and support, and what we can do in order to be ready for the challenge.

Having looked the problem in the face, determined our best response, done the footwork, and enlisted help, we can turn the ordeal and our performance over to the grace of a Higher Power.

Today, I trust that the same grace that has kept me going this far will lift me over future hurdles.

Being present is an expression of love.

When someone we care about is in distress, we may not know what to say. We'd like to make the hurt go away and set everything right, but we feel awkward and powerless.

Sometimes the greatest gift we can give each other is our presence, our attention. As we recover, we become more available emotionally to those we love, less preoccupied with craving and control, and less withdrawn and isolated. Having experienced the healing support of our Twelve Step groups, we can share our strength and hope by simply being there for someone else, whether or not that person is in the program.

We know that each of us must find his or her own answers. There are many times when, much as we'd like to, we can't fix the problems of our friends, children, parents, or other family members. What we can do is show them by our presence that we care and are on their side. We can spend time with them or, if we're geographically separated, we can call or write. And we can be confident that the same Higher Power that supports us is also supporting those we love.

My presence today can make a positive difference to someone dear to me.

*We can ask our Higher Power for
the gift of willingness.*

When we tried to use willpower to control what we ate, we got stuck, because some part of us was resisting. It's as though our will was divided, pushing in one direction while at the same time pulling in the opposite direction.

Step Three suggests we turn our will over to an integrating force that is stronger than we are. We give up self-will, and in exchange we are made willing to trust a Higher Power.

Willingness leads to healing. It allows us to follow the directions we receive from the quiet voice inside that speaks to our best interest. Willingness softens our old rigidity and erases *can't* and *won't* from our vocabulary. Willingness puts us in harmony with our spiritual promptings and in rhythm with the dance of recovery.

Today, I ask for the willingness to move to the rhythm of recovery.

If unmanageability strikes again,
it's time to review Step One.

Many of us take Step One again and again. That does not mean the program is failing for us. It means we are aware of the times when our recovery is precarious, and we know what to do when that happens.

Unmanageability may appear in various guises. We may bite off more than we can chew in terms of activities — we can binge on work, parties, even worthwhile community service projects. Our lives easily become unmanageable if we don't allow sufficient time and space for relaxation. Emotions become unmanageable when self-will runs riot, or conversely, when we don't take reasonable care of our own needs. And we know only too well the chaos that ensues when we lapse back into overeating or restricting.

Step One is there for us, a touchstone when events and feelings threaten to get out of hand. We can let go of the attempt to do everything, manipulate our emotions, or control other people. By admitting and accepting our areas of powerlessness and unmanageability, we become ready to receive help.

Staying close to Step One today will keep me safe.

Health is on our side.

By making a commitment to follow a reasonable food plan, we cooperate with the body's drive to be healthy. We have the opportunity to reverse as much as possible whatever damage may have been done by harmful eating patterns. Each day that we follow our plan, we are laying the groundwork for a healthy body.

Along with building a healthy body, our program of recovery fosters psychological and spiritual well-being. We believe that the Higher Power we invoke is directing us toward maximum development of our potential for total health — in intellect, body, emotions, and spirit. The forces of health are leading us away from compulsion, abuse, and neglect and into freedom, care, and respect.

By letting go of negative habits and ways of thinking, and by welcoming and using the new tools the program gives us for recovery, we unite with the power of health. Very soon, we begin to see and feel a positive difference.

I am committed today to cooperating with the forces of health, which are on my side.

We can take a positive lead.

When we are preoccupied with food and diets, we tend to take a passive role in our relationships with other people. We're more likely to act out our frustrations by using food destructively than by relating directly to the significant others in our lives in ways that lead to getting our needs met.

Sometimes we fall into the habit of letting other people make the suggestions, requests, and decisions. Our reaction may be to either blindly agree and then resent our compliance, or to categorically oppose the other person. Either way, we are reacting rather than taking a positive lead to ensure that our needs and desires are considered.

Touching base with our spiritual center helps us determine where it is we want to go. Then it's up to us to initiate the actions that will carry us toward those goals. Blaming someone else for our lack of progress keeps us stuck. Taking responsibility for the first move enhances our self-esteem and integrity.

Today, I will look for opportunities to initiate rather than react.

October

The longest day is only twenty-four hours.

Fortunately, we work on recovery one day at a time. However difficult the circumstances may seem, these twenty-four hours are the only ones we need be concerned with today. If we keep our attention focused on the present, the here and now, we can marshall the strength we need. It's when we project today's difficulties out into an indefinite future, magnifying them in our minds, that we begin to feel hopelessly inadequate.

Life doesn't intend us to cross bridges and scale mountains before we actually come to them Tomorrow's bridges and mountains, which loom so large today, will assume manageable proportions tomorrow. The strength we are given need only be adequate to the demands and challenges of today.

If we feel ourselves faltering, if we're tempted to retreat into using food destructively, we know where to turn for help. We can pick up the telephone, go to a meeting, read program literature. We're not alone. We have the support of the group and the strength of a Higher Power.

If today seems long, I will remember where to turn for help.

Don't cheat yourself —
life is to be enjoyed.

Although it's true that recovery enhances our ability to give to other people, we are the ones who benefit most. Eating too much or too little, which began as an attempt to feel better, eventually made us feel worse and robbed us of the enjoyment that life offers. As we recover from the eating disorder, we regain the capacity to experience joy, satisfaction, delight, sensual pleasure — all of the good things we were trading away for an addiction.

We settled for so much less than was available. By giving up our food obsession, we're back in the mainstream, open to enjoy people, places, ideas, feelings, activities, and experiences. Each day we reap new benefits.

When we let go of the circumstances over which we have no control, when we let the Steps be our guide, we realize there is no reason why we should not have our share of pleasure. We were standing in our own way, but we have moved aside so that we may receive life's blessings.

Recovery brings joy.

*Two secrets of a happy life: don't try
to control and don't complain.*

The wisdom of the ages is condensed for us in
the Twelve Steps. We have a surefire method for
achieving inner peace and serenity. First we sur-
render control to a Power greater than ourselves,
and then we accept whatever happens without
complaint.

Frustrated in our attempts to control outside
events and other people, we turned to food — eating it or not eating it — as an attempt to control
our own bodies instead. Our eating disorder was
a huge nonverbal complaint against the forces beyond our control. We probably did some verbal
complaining too.

Dealing with problems by controlling and complaining saps our energy and poisons our outlook.
The Steps show us a better way: relinquishing
self-will and allowing the God of our understanding to be in charge. Then, rather than uselessly
complaining, we can get on with our lives as we
are directed to from within.

----

*Today, I will try to steer clear of controlling
and complaining.*

Recovery is a journey.

With our decision to allow spiritual growth to take priority over our food obsession, we begin the journey of recovery. In the initial stages, our attention is probably focused on food plans and the twists and turns of daily abstinence. As we move along, we are concerned not only with issues of eating but with the broader challenges of living — meeting them directly without trying to use food and diets as a buffer. The further we progress on the journey of recovery, the more our scope expands to include the peaks and valleys of our total life experience.

On the journey, we may encounter unexpected delays and detours, but our direction is clear: we are moving toward greater reliance on a Higher Power and, paradoxically, greater freedom. Temporary setbacks need not deter us from our goal. All we need do is pick up where we left off and let the Steps direct us forward.

Knowing we are on a journey assures that we will not become stagnant or complacent. New challenges keep us on the move. When we connect with the spiritual core of our lives, new growth is always possible.

I am ready for a new day on recovery's journey.

*When we don't get what we want,
we may get something better.*

The closing of the door on a cherished dream is hard to accept. We lose out on a promotion or are rejected by someone we love—life seems unfair, and we fail to understand how a Higher Power could possibly be on our side.

Doors close — each one of us knows how that feels — but other doors eventually open. Keeping our spirits up and our faith strong during the interim is our challenge. We want to resist the "what's the use?" attitude that undermines recovery. If the opening of those other doors were to depend solely on our own efforts, we might have cause for discouragement and pessimism, but fortunately this is not the case. Experience teaches us that some doors we cannot open ourselves; instead, they are opened to us when we are ready.

The perspective of time clarifies our interpretation of events that at close range might seem disastrous. We lose out on one job, but after a time we're offered a better one. Rejection opens the way to a new relationship. We can have faith that we will receive the good that is ours.

Today, I will have faith, knowing that doors will open for me when I am ready.

• OCTOBER 6 •

We don't have to expect the worst.

Preparing for the worst that can happen is a way of avoiding disappointment. If we are geared up for disaster, then anything less is a welcome surprise. We put up a strong defense in hopes we won't be caught off guard.

The disadvantage of anticipating disaster is that we expend large amounts of time and energy stewing over what may never come to pass. Like Chicken Little, we go around expecting the sky to collapse on top of our heads at any moment.

Look back over your last few months. How many things that could have gone wrong actually did? How much energy are you using now to worry about the future?

We can save ourselves much needless anxiety by expecting positive outcomes. But how do we give up our dire predictions? The same way we gave up our obsession with food and being thin — by relying on the Power that keeps the sky in place to also keep us in place.

I will expect positive outcomes today.

"Choose to" works better than
"have to."

As we grow in recovery, we may discover that the "have to" part of our lives is not as extensive or as rigid as our compulsions led us to believe. We can begin to see that in most cases, "have to" can be discarded in favor of "choose to." Most of us find "choose to" preferable because it gives us freedom and dignity.

We don't have to overeat, we don't *have to* binge, we don't *have to* starve ourselves. We can *choose to* eat three moderate meals each day because that makes us feel good. We don't *have to* work, exercise, or play to the point of exhaustion. We can *choose to* set reasonable limits. We don't *have to* see everything and go everywhere and do everything that comes along. We can be selective and *choose* how we will spend our time and energy and how we will allocate our resources. We can also choose our friends.

Recovery restores our power of choice. We are responsible to ourselves and to our Higher Power for the choices we make, but we are no longer trapped by compulsions.

Happily, I'm free to make choices today.

*Resentments are burdens we don't
need to carry.*

Carrying resentments as part of the day's baggage puts a heavy load on our spirits. Bitterness,
anger, and hate poison our outlook and are
reflected back on us. So often the roots of these
negative feelings lie buried in the past, but their
toxic effects wreak havoc in the present.

Our program has been termed a selfish one. We
take care of ourselves by letting go of resentments
and by making amends to those whom we have
harmed. In this way, we can be rid of the feelings
that depress our spirits and interfere with our
present relationships.

If I cling to bitterness and hate, I undoubtedly
hurt myself more than anyone. If I allow these
emotions to fester, my abstinence will be in danger. How much better to put the burden down so
that my spirit can soar and I can get on with my
life!.

*Just for today, I will not burden myself with
resentments.*

Life is too short for perfectionism.

Perhaps if we had an infinite amount of time on this earth, we could eventually learn how to be perfect. But because we have a limited life span, it is more realistic to accept our imperfections and enjoy ourselves in spite of them.

Perfectionism was part of the problem many of us had with food. We thought we had to be the best, the brightest, the most popular, the thinnest. We used food as consolation for not meeting the impossibly high expectations others had for us or we had for ourselves.

We can do ourselves a huge favor, and those we love a huge favor, by letting go of unrealistic expectations. Our program promotes the development of humility and acceptance. It teaches us that we can like and respect ourselves and others even though neither we nor they are perfect. Self-esteem and perfectionism are mutually exclusive. Here's to self-esteem!

I will not waste this precious day by trying to be perfect.

It's okay to be spontaneous.

We're getting in touch with our feelings — so what do we do with them? Our eating disorders interfered with expressing them. If we were anorexic, we tended to be rigid and inhibited, overly controlled. If we were bulimic, our impulsiveness probably got us into trouble. If we struggled with compulsive overeating, we may have been rigid or impulsive, or swung back and forth between both extremes.

Many of us grew up under pressure to conform to how our parents expected us to feel or what our peers urged us to do. If we were frequently criticized or made to feel out of step, we gave up our spontaneous wishes and ideas in favor of the compliance that would bring approval.

Now that we have reclaimed responsibility for our feelings and actions, we can follow our internal promptings and see where they lead. We can allow ourselves to cry, even if "big people" don't. We can stop and pick wildflowers. We can sing off key. Avoiding the extremes of rigid control and irresponsible impulsiveness, we're learning how to be comfortably spontaneous.

More and more, my program gives me the freedom to be myself.

Contentment is an inside job.

To be content is to be at peace with oneself and in harmony with one's surroundings. Contentment is something no one else can give us, no matter how much that person might desire to do so. If I am to be content, I myself must be the agent.

In the quest for contentment, our first impulse is often that of trying to change outside circumstances, including other people. An attractive idea perhaps, but usually not feasible. The sooner we realize that the only person, place, or thing on which we can effect a lasting change is us, the better our chances of finding contentment.

Although we can't control other people or the world at large, we can make choices about where we want to be, with whom we want to be, and how we want to be, based on our inner promptings. Contentment does not come from the outside, in the form of over- or undereating, relationships, or material things. Contentment comes from the inside, from knowing ourselves and our Higher Power, and from accepting who we are and where we are on our journey of recovery.

Today, I will let my inner voice lead the way to contentment.

Keep the communication lines open.

As long as we are willing to listen and talk, there's hope for a relationship. It's when we shut down communication, because of fear, anger, or apathy, that we close the door to understanding. If we back away from encountering another person and hide in food, diets, purges, or other forms of escape, then we decrease our chances of growing with another in a relationship.

Conflicts often run deep, and the differences may seem overwhelming and insurmountable. Ignoring the problem, refusing to talk, or letting ourselves become distracted might appear easier than communicating. But these are not solutions. The problem remains. Often we don't even know what the problem is until we sit down and talk about it.

We can disagree and still keep talking. We can allow the other person to express his or her feelings and ideas. Sometimes just being heard is enough to defuse a potentially volatile situation. Sometimes it isn't. Regardless, we can cultivate the courage and sensitivity to communicate honestly and constructively with those we love.

Today, I am willing to communicate.

*Being obsessed with food is
a waste of time.*

When we think about how much time — in total — we've spent practicing our eating disorder, it can be an impressive figure. Many of us have spent years being obsessed with calories, diets, binges, purges, scales, laxatives, exercise, how clothes fit, and whatever else went along with our particular eating-disorder ritual. The entire process was extremely time-consuming.

Some of us come to realize that we possibly could have brought up another child or prepared for another career or pursued a hobby quite seriously with only a small portion of the time and energy we spent on our food obsession. It's amazing how much gets done when overeating and undereating have no place on our agendas.

Today, we may be tempted to pull the end of a string that we know will begin to unravel our abstinence and plunge us back into the chaos and unmanageability of our preoccupation with food. If this happens, we can stop to realize that there is a world of things we'd really rather be doing with our time.

The hours of today are mine, as long as I don't give them to my food obsession.

Paying attention makes us feel good.

Now that we're out of the food fog, we can pay attention to what's going on around us. We can especially give our attention to the people around us. As we give others our interest, concern, and caring, we feel better about ourselves.

Our moods affect others. When we're relaxed and take time to share a few moments of friendly conversation, we are usually rewarded with an affirming response. When we neglect to let someone close to us know that we care, we miss an opportunity to build a warm, supportive relationship. Being too busy or too preoccupied with our own concerns cuts us off from the interpersonal nourishment most of us need every day, many times a day.

Whatever we do, alone or with other people, it is most satisfying when we give it our full attention. We can train ourselves to concentrate on the here and now so that we reap enjoyment from each contact and activity.

Wherever I am today, I will pay attention to the people who cross my path.

The enemy is fear.

Self-centered fear paralyzes us and takes us hostage. The dread of losing something dear to us or not getting what we think we should have grips us with doubt and uncertainty. Our confidence evaporates, and we forget the Higher Power that provides us each moment with what we need.

Fear saps our strength. It gets in the way of developing our talents. It keeps us busy warding off imaginary disasters. It sends us in search of relief, and we may become addicted to false solutions such as overeating, purging, or restricting.

The real solution to fear is love. Love lifts us out of the whirlpool of self-centered anxiety and allows us to flow with the gentle current of goodness and health.

Fear is a formidable enemy. The Twelve Steps provide us with a proven strategy for overcoming it. We turn to a Power greater than ourselves, and we receive the gifts of faith, hope, and love.

If fear attacks me today, I will use the Steps to find real relief.

Action strengthens belief.

Our belief in a Higher Power, in the force of good, becomes stronger as we act on it. Until we are willing to trust the God of our understanding for guidance and support in specific instances, our belief is abstract and untried. It is when we earnestly seek to know our Higher Power's will for us in a concrete situation, and then act accordingly, that our trust becomes solid.

Frequently, we are not willing to make a leap of faith and rely on a Power greater than ourselves until we have exhausted our own resources and hit bottom. Then, because we have nowhere else to turn, we turn to the God of our understanding.

At that point of desperation, many of us have received new strength and support. We look back and remember how our Higher Power came through for us in the past when we had the courage to act with faith and trust. We will act again, according to our inner guidance, and our belief will grow stronger.

Today, the process of coming to believe continues for me as I take concrete action based on my understanding of my Higher Power's will for me.

You are the hero of your life.

Each of us plays the starring role in the drama that is our life. We co-create the script, along with our Higher Power. Sometimes we forget our lines, and so we improvise as best we can. We are heroes, each of us, as we move through the events of the day, refining our character and using our gifts to shape the action of every scene.

We can each be a hero in the drama of recovery. To the casual observer, what we do and say may not appear to be at all heroic. But we — as insiders who are only too well acquainted with our individual limitations — can appreciate and applaud a difficult decision or action.

When we accept our role in life, when we pledge to use our energies to do the best we can, and when we rely on our Higher Power for guidance and support, we will be well on our way toward recovering.

I can be a hero today, even if it doesn't show.

•OCTOBER 18•

The name of the game is service.

What can I do for someone else today? If I keep this question firmly before me, I will not get lost in futile activities such as feeling sorry for myself. Nor will I experience frustration when I once again realize that the world does not revolve around me.

Recovering and giving service go hand in hand. It is by learning compassion for others and devoting ourselves to finding ways to help that we escape an unhealthy preoccupation with self and put our energies and abilities to constructive use. Service to other people validates our own strength and gives us the satisfaction of knowing that we can make a positive difference.

We begin our recovery by being receivers. We absorb the experience, strength, and hope of those who have found a way to physical, emotional, and spiritual health through the Twelve Steps. To continue the process of getting well, we give back to others in order to promote our common growth. In this program, we measure our wealth not by what we have but by what we have given away.

The service I give today measures the strength of my recovery.

*Underneath the packaging, we're
not so different after all.*

Some of us hid our eating disorder from family
and friends for many years. Even when we and
they knew, denial seemed easier than confrontation. But it wasn't. Not really. Denial meant that
we lived a life of pretense, trying to prevent our
hurt from showing.

Healing begins when we can talk about the
pain. We come together with others in a Twelve
Step group, and we learn that our individual problems are not unique. We are not strange or weird.
The details of our stories differ, but the main
themes are amazingly similar — low self-esteem,
a feeling of lack of control, the compulsion to
overachieve, compliance, an obsession with food
and weight, mood swings, perfectionism, isolation. We understand each other immediately and
know we're not alone.

And this is our strength. When we share our
troubles and help each other find solutions, what
seemed impossible gets done, with help from our
friends and our Higher Power. Together we can
do what we cannot do alone.

*I am supported today by program friends who
understand me.*

We need not fear the dance of life.

We are not meant to be spectators, watching other people have fun. We are meant to be participants in the dance of life. Our obsession with food and diets meant we focused our attention on ourselves rather than on the dance going on around us. In recovery, we gain the confidence to step out and move, taking our place with the other dancers as active participants in the best life has to offer.

We can learn to flow with the shifting rhythms and patterns of life's dance. As we come to accept and enjoy our bodies, we get over the fear of being awkward or inept or making a wrong move. Even if we don't get all the steps and motions just right, we can love what we do and trust that acting on our inner promptings will put us where we need to be when we need to be there.

As for the choreography of the dance, that's created by a Higher Power. And that's why we need not be afraid.

I will participate with confidence today in the dance of life.

*The strength we seek outside can
only come from within.*

We feel weak, and so we reach for a substance that we think will make us strong. Or we search for another person who appears to have the strength we feel we lack, and we cling to that person. Or we look to material wealth, which we think will give us security and make us strong.

We reach and search and look — but on the outside. For a time, we may think we've found the magic substance or the strong rescuer or the potent possessions, but then they let us down. And by that time, we may be harmfully hooked.

The Twelve Steps point the way to inner strength, the Higher Power that is spiritual. They lead us to a serenity and peace that is neither induced by a substance nor dependent on the idealized image of another person nor the result of acquiring wealth or possessions. When we go within, sincerely seeking to get in touch with our own source of strength, we will not be disappointed.

I will look inside today for the strength that my Higher Power promises.

This day will never come again.

Today's gifts are to be used and enjoyed today. If we formerly practiced putting life on hold because our weight wasn't ideal or because something else wasn't quite right, it's time for a change. No longer are we in the business of fantasy and procrastination. We have a program of action that enables us to appreciate the concrete benefits of each day.

If there is something we want to do — whether it's for us or for someone else — if there are words we want to say to a loved one or feelings we wish to express, the time is now. We can take advantage of today's opportunity rather than wait to see if a better one will come along tomorrow. Tomorrow is fiction. Today is real.

Because today only happens now, it is precious. It is rarely pure joy, but the problems of today are manageable if we stay in the present and rely on a Higher Power. When we come to the end of these twenty-four hours, we want to be able to say we did the best we could and we thoroughly appreciated our blessings.

I will fully enjoy today's gifts.

*Readiness is a precondition
for change.*

If we earnestly and conscientiously apply the tools of our program, we are certain to experience positive change. We are promised new freedom and happiness and assured that a Higher Power can and will remove our negative characteristics.

The question is, are we ready to change? If we hang on tightly to self-will, resentments, fear, mistrust, and all the other weaknesses that get in our way, our Higher Power has a tough time prying us loose. We must be prepared to let go and open ourselves to new possibilities if the change we seek is to occur.

Along with taking a daily inventory, we can cultivate the readiness to abandon our counterproductive tendencies and try something new. In this way, we cooperate with the force for positive growth that lies within each of us. We cannot command or control this force, but we can learn to be responsive to it.

Today, I am ready for positive change. I will be responsive to inner nudges that move me in that direction.

*Abstinence keeps us on the cutting
edge.*

When we give up our food obsession, we stop
retreating from life's challenges and turn our energies toward forging ahead. Abstinence gives us
the clarity we need to define our goals, and abstinence gives us the motivation to achieve them.
We stay on the cutting edge, alert to our inner signals, and empowered to move forward in the
direction of fulfillment.

We learn how to eat so that food does not control our lives. Then we can apply the same techniques to other areas where we wish to make
progress. If we're looking for a job, we can make
a daily plan for conducting the search. If we want
to meet new people, we can set a schedule for carrying out the campaign. Abstinence keeps us
moving toward our goals rather than retreating
into food.

Our Twelve Step philosophy undergirds whatever we do. From contact with a Higher Power
comes purpose and direction. From maintaining
abstinence comes the energy and motivation to
persevere in spite of difficulties.

---

*By maintaining abstinence today, I will make
progress.*

Are we strong enough to be gentle?

Recovery makes us strong. We may not be aware of increasing strength on a daily basis, but when we look back on where we came from, we can see how far we've progressed on our journey. As long as we continue to rely on a Higher Power instead of food or diets, our strength will continue to increase.

The stronger we are internally, the more gentle we can be with those whose lives we touch. In our emotional and physical dependency, we could not afford to be gentle with others. Our demands on them (and on ourselves) were harsh, since our needs were so great. For some of us, bingeing and temper tantrums went hand in hand. Others of us were manipulative in quieter, but equally destructive ways.

When we're strong enough to accept ourselves in spite of our mistakes and imperfections, we can extend the same tolerance and gentleness to those around us. The Twelve Step way of life leads us to this kind of strength. It enhances all of our relationships and helps those we love to grow.

One of my goals today is to combine gentleness with strength.

Food is not the problem.

What we eat or don't eat is not really the problem. Our eating disorders have to do with what food and weight mean to us and how we feel about our bodies. No amount of food and no amount of dieting will make up for low self-esteem and other inner problems.

As we recover, we learn to give food its proper place in our lives as nourishment for our bodies. When we stop being obsessive about weight and dieting, we can deal constructively with the issues underlying our eating disorders.

We have problems; everyone does. Eating and dieting became a sideshow, distracting us from the real issues we needed to face. Now we are in the main tent where we can concentrate on the people, events, and feelings that are significant to us. We can change. We can grow. We can find real solutions to our real problems.

Today, I will remember that food is not the problem, and food is not the solution.

Why me?

We wonder why we have a problem with food, why we restrict out of fear of a normal-size body, why we can't eat like other people do. We ask these questions, because it doesn't seem fair that we should have to struggle so hard with what appears to be simple and natural for other people.

The answers may not be readily available. Since eating disorders are complex illnesses, it's difficult to identify a specific cause. Even if we knew exactly why we have a problem with food, we would still be confronted with the task of doing something about it. Instead of why me, the question is what next.

To this question, the program has answers. We follow the Steps, we make contact with a Higher Power, and we embark on a new way of life. Instead of feeling sorry for ourselves, we appreciate the fact that recovery is possible and that in the process we can become strong, probably stronger than we would have been even if we had never had a food problem.

Today, I will do what's next in my recovery.

Recovery unearths buried talents.

Self-expression flourishes in recovery. The talents that were hidden when we were obsessed with food and diets can now be uncovered and developed. As we come to know ourselves better, we discover what we truly enjoy doing, and we learn how to claim and develop our natural abilities.

Recovery frees us from the inhibiting attitude of perfectionism. If we like to sing, we can find ways to enjoy that without expecting to meet professional standards of performance. As our bodies become healthier, we may discover athletic abilities we never knew we had. Perhaps we have a talent for making people feel comfortable — how many opportunities there are to use this gift!

On our journey of recovery, we find hidden treasures that enrich our lives and the lives of those we love. If we dig deeply and polish our gifts with patience, we will be rewarded with the satisfaction that comes from developing our inborn talents.

Today, I will search for my own buried treasure.

With a Higher Power, it's safe to be fluid.

Rigid systems were what we clung to when we felt alone and uncertain. Now that we're connected to a source of strength beyond ourselves, we can let go of compulsive patterns of thinking and acting. We can respond to the flow of life, trusting we will be carried along on the stream of goodness.

Our safety and security lie not in the systems we concoct and not in the material props we collect. They lie in our ability to respond creatively to the opportunities offered to us each day.

The Steps of our program are suggested, not mandated, and they may be adapted to our individual needs. Recovery encourages flexibility. We learn to trust our instincts, confident that our deep desires will lead us to satisfaction. We learn to trust the God of our understanding to give us the intuitive knowledge that keeps us on course.

I will stay clear of rigid systems today, so that I can flow with my inner currents.

*Recovering means we no longer have
a primary relationship with food.*

Once upon a time we used food and diets to
satisfy emotional needs. Now we are learning better ways of filling these needs, ways that mean
building healthy relationships with people.

We need to find out what we want from our
relationships and what we are prepared to give.
These are important questions. If our relationship
with food and diets is no longer primary, what
takes its place?

We need to be able to share with others our feelings, plans, hopes, disappointments — the stuff of
everyday life. We need friends who will give us affection, support, encouragement. And we need to
give in return. We need to ask ourselves how
much time, energy, and attention we are prepared
to invest in nurturing our primary relationships
with other people.

As we shift our emotional focus from food and
diets to people, we learn how to balance our
needs for intimacy and separateness, when to
come close and when to move away. We are in the
arena of real life.

*My primary relationships today will be with peo-
ple, not food.*

The strongest and best security is love.

When we love, we feel at home in the world. We are buoyant, confident, and filled with faith in the power of goodness. We experience the inner security that comes with stepping away from center stage and learning to care about other people. Egocentric fears diminish. The love we share nourishes our spirit.

None of us is able to exist as a self-contained unit. Because we know we need other people, we are anxious and fearful when we lack close, loving relationships. We need friends we can depend on, and this implies being dependable in return.

Material security goes only so far. It is not enough. The love we give comes back to us in the form of emotional and spiritual security. Grounded in this love, we cease to crave the substitutes that not only did not work but that eventually created the insecurity of addiction.

My true security today lies in the love I receive from a Higher Power and share with others.

November

When we forgive others, we forgive ourselves.

Holding grudges is hazardous to our recovery. We need to let go of the past so that old resentments do not poison the present. This is hard to do. When we feel we have been injured, our instincts urge us to strike back in retaliation.

Nobody wins that way. There are two sides to every quarrel. We cannot coerce another person to forgive us for the harm we have done, but we can forgive the injuries we have suffered.

Forgiveness frees us from past hurts. We do not need to seek consolation in excess food or try to numb the hurt by starving. When we are able to forgive others, we can also forgive ourselves for our part in the conflict. By allowing others to make mistakes, we allow ourselves to err, make amends, and start again.

If I am holding grudges from the past today, may I allow myself the freedom of forgiveness.

*We can trust life to unfold the way
it's supposed to.*

Anxiety about getting the results we want is hard to shake. Whether it's meeting a prospective mother-in-law or interviewing for a job, it's not the situation itself that creates pressure, it's our anxiety about getting the results we want that pressures us.

Our program of recovery suggests that we make our plans and leave the results to our Higher Power. If we're not intent on controlling the outcome of events, it's much easier to let go of addictive patterns of behavior. We can relax and let life run its course without trying to determine what that course will be. Whatever the outcome, we can continue to count on the support of a Higher Power.

If we're turned down for one job, chances are we will have another opportunity to be useful. If one person doesn't seem to like us, probably someone else will. Limited as our perspective is, we can't always know what's best in the long run. That's where faith and trust take over.

How many of my anxieties today can I turn over to the God of my understanding?

Today is another chance.

Maybe abstinence wasn't so good yesterday. Perhaps we didn't handle a tense situation at work very well. Maybe we had an argument with a family member and said things we wish we hadn't.

We make mistakes and errors in judgment. Emotions carry us away, and we lose our balance and perspective. Can we forgive ourselves and start again? Can we also forgive the other people involved? If so, we have another chance. The unfortunate episode can be a learning experience — next time we'll know what to do.

Although we have the guidelines for recovery, we don't always follow them. When we get off the track, we don't need to waste time and energy criticizing ourselves or others. Instead, we can begin again with this new day and profit from the experience that went before it. Recovery is now.

I will take advantage of today's new chance.

The sharp edges of my personality are
my hunger for love and affection.

When I appear to be hard and brittle, I am actually asking for care and concern. I fear I may not get it and so, in advance, I put up a hard shell of defense against possible hurt. This, of course, makes me less lovable.

Many of us carry unmet needs from way back. Love and affection may have been in short supply when we were growing up. At one point we used food to compensate, or we starved ourselves in protest.

There are better ways of filling our needs. We don't have to automatically assume we won't get the love we want, and we don't need to grow spikes on our exterior as armor against disappointment. All around us are fellow human beings who also need love and affection. If we will take the chance of softening our defenses, we will invite the warmth we crave. If we will move toward others and be sensitive to their unmet needs, we can begin to satisfy our hunger for closeness.

Today, I will allow my sharp edges to soften.

Wanted: a program of exercise for spiritual muscles.

If we don't use our spiritual muscles, they get flabby. It's so easy to let ourselves be inundated by concerns with what we have to do, what we want to buy, what we'd like to achieve, and other daily preoccupations. Then we find ourselves feeling frazzled, tired, and lacking the vitality that comes when we are spiritually fit.

The Twelve Steps outline a program of spiritual exercise. As with any other exercise regimen, regular practice is essential. We may have a tendency to find other things to do, or slack off when we get bored, but there is a built-in monitor: when we neglect our spiritual program, unmanageability sounds an alarm.

The beauty of spiritual exercise is that it can be done at any time and in any place. The only equipment necessary is an attitude of willingness and openmindedness. At any moment during the day, we can recall our contact with a Higher Power and stretch our spiritual muscles.

Becoming spiritually fit is my desire. I will use today's opportunities for exercise.

To be alive is to be hungry.

Our appetite for life is good. It keeps us reaching, growing, enjoying, yearning to fulfill our potential. When our basic needs are satisfied, our hunger propels us to search for more elaborate gratification.

Here is where we often run into trouble. Instead of progressing through the hierarchy of needs to the spiritual level, we get stuck in an attempt to make quantity — more things, more people, more activity — substitute for quality. And quantity alone is never enough.

It's good that we're hungry. Our appetite motivates us to feed our body in a healthy way and also to feed our mind, heart, and spirit. Our needs pyramid, and our hunger leads us beyond quantity to the quality experiences that fill our emptiness. We read, we share, we love, we pray, we listen, we accomplish, we dance, we feast on the fullness of life.

Today, I will direct my appetite to quality experiences.

We don't need crutches.

We are unique and wonderful people. We have weaknesses, yes, and we also have strengths beyond our imagining. We can meet the day without the prop of food we don't need or an overly restrictive diet. We can put away these crutches and just be ourselves.

Perhaps we needed a crutch at one time. We got used to it, and even though it was in our way and slowed us down, we were afraid to venture forth without it. Gradually, the crutch began to control our movements and take over our life. We became its slave.

Then we were invited to consider the possibility of a Higher Power that would eliminate our need for a crutch. Intrigued, we began to practice relying on this Higher Power in concrete ways on a daily basis.

We are learning how to walk again. Scary sometimes, without the old props, but Step by Step we're on our way to recovery.

Just for today, I will put away the crutches I no longer need and rely on my Higher Power.

*If we see only ourselves, it's a very
lonely world.*

We can learn the difference between taking
care of ourselves positively and being so nega-
tively self-centered that we are forced into soli-
tary confinement, where we dry up for lack of
genuine interchange.

We should know who we are. But we should
also know who our neighbor is, and our friend,
sister, boss, or child. To know other people and
see beneath the exterior they present, we need to
be comfortable enough with ourselves so we can
relax and look and listen. We also need to be humble enough to realize we can learn from someone
else and benefit from the gifts she or he brings to
the relationship.

With recovery comes new empathy and sensitivity. As self-will loosens its grip, we are open to
the intuitive knowledge that enhances our inter-
actions with those around us. Since our vision is
less clouded by the problems of addiction, we can
see others more clearly and understand them better. Recovery offers us a way out of loneliness into
companionship and community.

*I will use my empathy to deepen my understand-
ing of those who cross my path today.*

Quality moments grace recovery.

We don't command them, nor do we produce them, but we can be alert and sensitive to the timeless moments of pleasure and delight that grace our days unexpectedly. For many of us, these moments come most often when we turn our will over to a Power greater than ourselves.

The smile of recognition when we're with someone who intuitively understands exactly how we're feeling at a particular moment, the sense of calm and peace when we spend quiet time alone, a deep breath on a crisp fall morning — these are times when we're grateful to be getting better.

The special beauty of these gifts is that we don't bring them about by overachieving or being perfect. We just put one foot in front of the other, march along to the rhythm of our inner song, and reap the benefits of Twelve Step living.

I will savor today's unexpected moments of delight.

Commitment propels us in the direction we have chosen.

Commitment is the wind that fills our sails. It gets us going in the direction we want to move. Without commitment, we do a great deal of speculating and desiring, but we don't make much progress.

No matter what we want to do — learn a skill, find a job, recover from an eating disorder, build an enduring relationship with another person — commitment is the key. Whether we regard these goals as pleasant achievements or desire them passionately, until we commit ourselves to action, they will not become realities.

Commitment means channeling our energies toward a specific goal, saying yes to everything that supports that goal and no to everything that could detract from it. Commitment involves making a choice and following through. When we make a commitment to abstinence, to someone we love, to the work we want to accomplish, we release strength, energy, and enthusiasm. This propels us in the direction we want to move.

To what and whom am I committed today? What actions do my commitments require?

*Create a sense of serenity in your
life.*

Developing a sustaining sense of serenity requires time. Time to do the things we need to do without rushing. Time for meditation. Time for just being with ourselves and moving quietly from one task to another. In this way, we develop a deep core of serenity, which sustains us in times of stress and strain.

The next time you feel yourself getting upset, stop and connect with the core of serenity within you. Savor the peace and stillness you felt during quieter times. Remember that a Higher Power is in charge of your life. Consider the damage you may do to yourself and others by giving vent to your distress. Then test how it would feel to let go of the agitation and replace it with the serenity you have deep within you.

Take a few moments now to sit quietly and connect with your abiding sense of serenity. Be at peace.

In today's quiet times, I will create a core of serenity to draw from in the future.

Find a bucket and fill it with love.

If you ever played with a bucket at the beach, you discovered that you could fill it with water from the ocean, pour it out on the sand, and go back for more endlessly. The supply of water was enough for as many bucketsful as you desired.

The supply of love in this world is inexhaustible, but we sometimes neglect to fill our buckets. Or we forget to empty them. Unless we pour out the love we receive, we have no room in our buckets for more. We need buckets of love for ongoing recovery, and the more we have, the better — we can never have too many. Paradoxically, the way we keep the buckets full is by emptying them regularly. Then the ocean of love comes back with the tide and fills them up again.

Those of us who depend on a Higher Power believe that our love is ultimately replenished from a spiritual source. That's what makes the supply inexhaustible.

I will pour out my bucket of love many times today so it can be refilled.

Wholeness is our birthright.

Creation's intent is not that we should be sick but that we should be well and healthy. We cooperate with the power of healing and wholeness when we abstain from harmful ways of eating. Our bodies are restored to health.

Since body, mind, spirit, and emotions cannot be separated, we want the kind of healing that takes place on all levels. We want to be integrated, in touch with our feelings and able to act in our own best interest. You and I are meant to function as whole people.

If we are willing to get to know ourselves completely — our dreams and motivations, and even our dark side, the side of ourselves we don't like — we will have nothing to hide or deny. Knowing that a Higher Power accepts us just as we are, we can give ourselves the kind of total acceptance that leads to healing and peace.

My thoughts and actions today will promote my wholeness and integrity.

*Life requires only that we give
what we have.*

How do we summon up the courage not to run away from our own potential? It is tempting to try to escape the hard work of developing our abilities, to turn our backs on the challenges life presents and look for an easier way.

But if we don't use our strengths, we become bored, frustrated, and depressed. If we are obsessed with food and losing weight, we direct too much of our attention to what we eat and how we look, neglecting to develop our particular talents.

We're not expected to be superhuman or accomplish miracles. We can, however, be willing to face the demands of each day and try to meet them. We can only give what we have, but in the giving we find new strength and new gifts.

Whatever challenges today brings, I will try to recognize and apply the strengths and abilities I am given.

*Sometimes the heart understands
what baffles the mind.*

The heart has a wisdom that often eludes rational thought. A person's behavior may appear to be selfish or unreasonable unless we are able to intuitively sense what motivates it. If we look with eyes of love, we can understand and forgive defensive actions that are part of an effort to protect the self rather than to hurt another.

Taking our own inventory is good preparation for the development of an understanding heart. Admitting our mistakes helps us to be tolerant of another's weaknesses.

The logic of the heart cuts through complexities. If I love you, I give you the benefit of the doubt in the interest of our deepening relationship. I may not understand with my mind why you do what you do, but my heart can accept and respect you.

I will strive today to have an understanding heart.

Like it or not, we're on a journey.

Life doesn't stand still. It's on the move. The weather changes from one day to the next, and so does the scenery in our environment. And so do we.

When we come in contact with the Twelve Steps, we have an opportunity to make our journey a deeply meaningful one, one that is directed toward spiritual goals. We can make use of all the events in our lives — from the minor details of what clothes we wear to the major decisions about how we will relate to the members of our family. We can use everything that happens to fuel our progress.

Being on a journey means waking up in the morning and not knowing exactly how much ground we will cover today, or exactly what will happen along the way. Nevertheless, when we determine that our ultimate destination is spiritual growth as directed by a Higher Power, we have faith that whatever the day brings belongs in our itinerary.

It's a new day, so on with the journey!

*I don't want my concern for me to
block out my awareness of you.*

It's so easy for me to be completely preoccupied with how I feel, what kind of impression I think I'm making on you, how I want you to respond to me. When this happens, I lose my awareness of you, and there is no chance for dialogue. I-me-myself becomes a noisy monologue inside my head as well as outside my mouth, and I lose you. Then I'm lonely and unhappy.

Beneath our egocentricity is insecurity. If our sense of self-worth is low, we constantly try to convince self and others that we are smart, clever, talented, and good. Uncomfortable with the natural ebb and flow of conversation, we expend great effort trying to prove our worth, and we forget to listen to the other person.

The process of recovery punctures our inflated bubble of egotism. Learning to tune in and listen, we try less to impress someone else and more to understand him or her. The reward is dialogue.

I will lower my volume today so I can hear you.

*Getting high on life is the best
addiction.*

Addicted to life — this is the way we hope to be as we move ahead in our recovery. We give up the false highs that only too quickly let us down, and we choose instead the lasting satisfactions of healthy living, loving relationships, and useful work. We give up the fantasies and let ourselves become hooked on reality.

Being open and vulnerable to what life brings us each day is a challenge that leads to growth. Bingeing and purging, restricting and overeating — these are defenses we put between ourselves and the rough edges of real life. When we give up the defenses, we are more vulnerable to the hurt of rejection, the anxiety of risk, the sadness of loss. We also become more alive to the joy of love and friendship, the thrill of accomplishment, the beauty of the world around us.

The more we rely on a Higher Power, the less we need false highs and crippling defenses. A new world opens, which we may enter timidly at first but with increasing confidence as we become convinced that as we give to life, so life gives back to us.

Today, I will be open to whatever life brings.

When I'm comfortable with me, I'm comfortable with you.

I can't expect you to give me peace and serenity — they come from within, and they are nurtured by spiritual growth. If I'm uncomfortable with myself, not at peace, the tension spills over into my relationship with you, and nothing seems quite right.

We are each responsible for our own serenity. It develops out of knowing who we are and what we need, accepting our flaws along with our potential for positive change, and believing in the force for ultimate good. To be comfortable with ourselves requires that we face our inner tigers and stare them down. When we can enjoy our time alone without needing to escape into some form of distraction, we know serenity.

How comfortable I am when I'm with you depends on my level of self-esteem. When it's high and healthy, I can relate to you without demanding consciously or unconsciously that you make up for what I lack. The serenity I crave results from my own commitment to recovery through spiritual growth.

The inner work I do today will help nurture my relationships.

*In recovery, we find our natural
rhythm.*

Artificial highs and lows, bursts of energy, and
periods of lethargy went along with our eating
disorder. The binge-fast or binge-purge syn-
drome distorted our natural rhythms. We had
periods when we drove ourselves at breakneck
speed and other times when we moved through
life in slow motion.

Moderating our eating patterns is the first step
toward recovering a comfortable, natural rhythm
in life. We learn to pace ourselves — not too fast
and not too slow — and we discover how we
function best. When we stop bingeing at night,
we reclaim the mornings. When we're getting the
nutrition we need at regular intervals, we avoid
the lows of exhaustion.

Recovery puts us in touch with our own best
pace. We receive inner signals that tell us when it's
time to work or rest or play. And we develop the
confidence to follow these signals, respecting the
natural rhythm that orders our days.

---

*Today, I will keep time to the natural rhythm of
my body, mind, and heart.*

*The ability to work is one of
recovery's blessings.*

Some of us know what it is to lose the ability to function at work or at school because of an eating disorder. Others of us have been able to carry on, but with diminished effectiveness. Being obsessed with food and diets generally does not improve anyone's job performance.

What a joy to wake up in the morning clearheaded and ready to accomplish a useful task! Our work is our gift to the world and the expression of our special capabilities. Other people benefit from what we do, and we have the satisfaction of being able to produce and contribute.

Work provides structure and purpose to our lives. Since for most of us our job consumes a major portion of our time, it is important that what we do is congruent with who we want to be. If the job we have does not challenge us to use our abilities fully, we can consider a change. Perhaps the desired change can be incorporated into what we're already doing; perhaps we need to explore new options. Either way, we have the firm ground of recovery as a solid base of operation.

Today, I will use and enjoy my ability to work.

*When all else fails, take a nap or go
to bed early.*

Using food to give ourselves a push can be harmful. Most of us know only too well how turning to food for a quick pick-me-up can escalate out of control. We'd like to find a marvelous elixir that would safely boost our energy level whenever we need a lift, but so far we haven't discovered that magic potion.

We all know how much more difficult each task becomes when we're tired. Doesn't it make sense to stop, rest, and return to the task later, when we are refreshed and can handle it better? Our minds and bodies are the only ones we have. When we're feeling physically or mentally dull, it's time to rest instead of reaching for food.

Unnecessary food goes only so far. After the quick lift, we drop down lower than before and we crave another fix — more high-carbohydrate food.

Problems shrink when we are rested. After we've done all we can effectively do, it's time for a break.

*Today, I will replenish my energy with rest rather
than with unnecessary food.*

Following a food plan gives us new options.

When we decide on a healthy food plan, and when we do what we need to do to follow it — such as write it down and call a sponsor — we have the freedom to find new things to do with the day. With food and eating taken care of in a healthy way, we can get on with the rest of life.

Recovery from an eating disorder gives us options we did not have when so much of our time and attention were devoted to food and diet obsessions. Now that our bodies function for us instead of against us, our emotional energy is available for whatever we choose to do, and our spirit wakes up and sings.

We have opportunities we never had before — to study, build, play, work, enjoy, dream, love. When compulsion is lifted, our time and energy are released. We're no longer locked into old patterns of behavior — we are free.

I will follow my food plan today and take advantage of the new options that are available to me.

Gratitude is a way of life.

Saying thank-you from the heart makes us feel full. Perhaps we don't really know we have something until we express our thanks for it.

There are different levels of gratitude. There is the polite, automatic response when someone opens a door for us or the bank teller tells us to have a nice day. Simple, almost perfunctory, these acts of courtesy nevertheless add an element of grace to our daily transactions.

On a more personal level, saying thank-you often and sincerely to those we love keeps us from taking each other for granted. We all like to feel appreciated — how many relationships dry up because the people involved don't realize what they have?

Then there is the gratitude we feel toward the God of our understanding, the source of all the blessings we enjoy but do not create for ourselves. This thankfulness can be a part of every breath we take. As often as we remember the many gifts of every day, our emptiness is filled.

Today, I will replenish my supply of gratitude.

Some days, "hanging in there" is a
real accomplishment.

You wake up tired. There are problems at home
and problems at work. You try to fix the problems, but you seem to make them worse. Nothing
appears to go right.

This is the kind of day that used to send you
straight to the refrigerator or to a fast-food restau-
rant. Or you went to the other extreme and tried
to gain control by not eating at all, even though
you knew your weight was dangerously low.

None of us is immune from having one of these
kinds of days from time to time. That's why we
build up reserves that we can draw on to get us
through tough days. We make abstinence a habit,
so no matter how many problems we have, we
don't try to solve them with food — either eating
it or not eating it. We also make conscious contact
with a Higher Power a habit, so when everything
appears to be going wrong, we may be assured
that the disturbances are temporary and that we
will be given the help we need.

If today is tough, I will "hang in" and work my
program.

What happens to us is not as important as how we respond.

The external events of our lives are largely beyond our control. We do not choose our parents, our emotional environment, the historical period in which we live, our body type, or the flow of circumstances that shape our experience. These are givens. We do not select them, but we can choose how we will react to them, and in that choice lies our freedom and our responsibility.

Instead of complaining about the hand we've been dealt, we can concentrate on playing it well. This is the way we exercise our freedom. What might appear to be random chance can take on meaning and purpose as we delve for insight and use our deficiencies as opportunities for growth.

Our responsibility is to do the best we can with what we have where we are. And we don't do it alone. We have help in learning how best to respond. We have a support group, we have a Higher Power, and we have an inner guide if we will listen for direction.

Today, I will remember that the what of my life is not as important as the how.

Taking the first step helps bridge the gulf between our dreams and our accomplishments.

Whether the project is cleaning the garage, building a cathedral, or recovering from an eating disorder, plans must be translated into action. In order to arrive at our destination, we must begin the trip. We can read hundreds of college catalogs, but it's when we register for a course, buy a textbook, and begin to study that we are on our way to a degree.

Two factors inhibit our beginning a project. The first is lack of clear motivation, and the second is fear of failure. If we don't really want to do something, it's hard to get started. So, if motivation is a problem, we may need to reconsider our choice of projects.

As for fear of failure, this may be something that we step over and around as we move forward. It is not a good reason for aborting a dream. If, in spite of fear of failure, we make a beginning, we will find that the fear shrinks with every step we take. Action is the catalyst. We learn how to do something by doing it.

I will take the first step toward accomplishing a dream today by getting started.

Share the wealth.

We're finding solutions to our problems with food and to the underlying issues of living. We're finding a wealth of understanding and support from others who are recovering and from the spiritual reservoir that links us with all humanity. By sharing our insights, experience, strength, and hope, we keep our recovery alive and ongoing.

Step Twelve reminds us that we have a message to carry and a way of life that works. We have riches to share, and in the sharing, these riches increase. We can help someone else find the way out of the misery of food abuse and in so doing strengthen our own recovery.

As our lives become richer under the management of a Higher Power, we discover that the principles of our program function beautifully, no matter what the situation. We can share the wealth with those whose lives we touch whether or not they are part of the recovering community. Our job is to carry the message — who responds and how is up to our Higher Power.

I will remember today that I have wealth to share.

After abstinence comes more abstinence.

Our goal is to make eating for health a way of life, an ingrained habit that is natural and comfortable. We choose to eat appropriate amounts of the foods that make us feel strong and alert. This is no hardship. This is doing ourselves a favor.

Abstinence means we avoid manipulating our intake of calories to produce a high. Sounds boring? Not really. Overeating and bingeing were boring, and so was restricting, since they cut us off from so many more interesting things we could have been doing. When our principal means of gratification centered around food or weight loss, life was limited indeed.

Knowing that abstinence can continue as a given part of the day's routine prompts us to look for interest, stimulation, and excitement beyond the narrow confines of over- or undereating. We come out of our shell, seek contact with people, and find challenging activities to add zest to our lives. More abstinence makes it all possible. More abstinence means more freedom and more fun.

I am thankful I can continue to choose abstinence today.

*I'd rather feel lousy than not feel
at all.*

We all have down days, times when we are discouraged, depressed, blue. A disappointment comes our way — something we had hoped for falls through, someone we had counted on lets us down — and we feel lousy.

When you come home in the evening and are feeling down, you have to decide what you'll do. You know that eating food you don't need may blot out your disappointment temporarily, but how will you function tomorrow morning if you binge — and maybe purge — tonight? You also know that restricting your intake below what your body requires may numb your bad feelings now, but what will happen to your energy level?

We can develop the courage to experience our down times, the patience to wait them out, and the resourcefulness to find something useful to do while we wait. We can remind ourselves that even bad feelings are better than no feelings. Our downs are part of being alive.

*If I feel depressed today, I will go into the feeling
and learn from it.*

December

*I have faith that the sun will rise
tomorrow.*

Without faith, we would probably come to a grinding halt. We expect the water to boil, the car to start, our home to be there when we return at night. We expect people to answer when we say hello.

Each day I proceed with reasonable confidence that the mechanics of my life will follow their prescribed course. Otherwise, I wouldn't make it out the front door.

So much for the mechanics. What about the big questions? Will I be able to find a new job if I need one? Is my daughter marrying the right man? Are we headed for a nuclear disaster?

I can worry about a multitude of big and little questions. I can become paralyzed with doubt, or I can try to ease the doubt and fear with food or restricting. But there is another alternative. I can trust that the universe is a friendly place, a place where I belong and where I have a role to play. I can have faith that just as the sun will rise, so will I be given what I need each day.

If it's cloudy today, I will have faith that the sun is still there.

*True commitment comes
from the heart.*

We can make a commitment with our minds and dutifully follow through, at least for a while. We can will to keep our promises, but aren't we only too familiar with the limitations of willpower? The kind of commitment that grasps us where we live and becomes an integral part of our deepest desire comes from the heart.

Whether the commitment is to a person, a cause, or an endeavor, love provides the glue. Our commitment to abstinence is only as strong as our love for self, body, and the feeling we have when we follow our food plan. Without that driving power of emotion, resolutions about what we will or will not eat fall flat and disintegrate.

A commitment from the heart brings us into spiritual territory. Here we become aware of what means most to us. Here our dedication to whom and what we love, and how we express that love, receives its staying power.

Today, I will lead with my heart.

*A positive attitude will create
opportunity.*

Although we can't control events or other people, we can decide what our attitude will be. And
the attitude we choose today will have a decisive
impact on the opportunities that become available to us.

We probably won't get what we want and need
if we decide in advance that we're incapable or
unworthy of receiving it. But just as gloom and
doom breed more of the same, an optimistic outlook invites a positive response.

Perhaps we have allowed past disappointments
to color our hopes in somber shades; thus, we
operate on the theory that if we don't expect anything, we won't be hurt or let down. We may
avoid a few popped balloons that way, but how
many promising opportunities do we forgo in the
process?

We don't know what today will bring in the
way of new knowledge, challenges, or problems.
We do know that if we approach each experience
positively, it can hold a promising opportunity
for us.

Today, I will expect good things.

*Freedom and discipline are two
sides of the same coin.*

The kind of freedom we sought through eating according to undisciplined impulse and whim turns out not to be freedom but a constricting bond of compulsion. We discover that without discipline, real freedom is not possible.

Accepting the discipline of a food plan offers liberation from what for many of us had become the tyranny of impulse. When we were clinging to mistaken ideas of what would satisfy, we were digging ourselves deeper into the sandtrap of dependency. Yes, we ate what we wanted to eat when we wanted to eat it, but it exacted an exorbitant price. What we had was not freedom but slavery to unhealthy habits.

The freedom we seek — freedom to function at our best, to enjoy life, to create, to love — this freedom comes as we tame our impulses. Healthy discipline does not destroy spontaneity. It provides the framework within which spontaneity can safely flourish.

I will embrace a healthy discipline today, in order to be free.

One way to avoid mistakes is to do nothing.

If I'm afraid of saying the wrong thing, I can, of course, say nothing. Sometimes this may be a good idea, but if it is carried to an extreme, communication languishes. If I'm afraid of looking foolish on the tennis court, I can refuse to play, but I won't enjoy or improve my game. If I'd like to write a novel but fear it won't be any good, I can decide not to begin, which ensures that I will not write a bad novel.

Fear paralyzes us: inactivity may begin as a defense against failure, but it becomes a millstone that sinks our hope for success.

When we picked up the Twelve Steps of recovery, we began to do something. However halting our efforts, we embarked on a program of decision and action. We became willing to make mistakes and try again. What would happen if a child learning to walk refused to risk falling down? There is a child in each of us that has the capacity to learn and grow — and that child learns by doing, in spite of fear.

When I do something that is important to me today, I will feel affirmed, even if it turns out to have been a mistake.

Life is meant to be lived and savored.

Life invites us to a banquet, a smorgasbord, a feast. How sad if we decline the invitation! Tragedy lies not in the fact that we all must die but in that some of us never really live our lives to the fullest. We allow our hopes, dreams, and talents to expire while we continue to breathe in and out. We say we're too busy to go to the banquet, or we select only a small sample from the bountiful feast.

The banquet of life is so much more than food. Those of us with eating disorders know that food is important. We're learning how much we need so we can enjoy not only the food but also the rest of the feast.

If we're placing unnecessary limits on our selections from all that life offers, we can seek friends or professionals who will help us broaden our choices. Our Higher Power works through the people who invite us to share the feast.

I will accept today's invitation to the banquet of life.

Don't say yes when you mean no.

Those of us with eating disorders are often people-pleasers. We say what we think people want to hear, because we want them to like us and be happy.

We get ourselves into big trouble by saying yes when we mean no. At someone's urging, we sign up for something we don't want to do and then resent the time we spend carrying out the project. Or we accept an invitation when we'd rather not go but don't want to hurt the other person's feelings by saying no.

As our self-esteem grows, we give ourselves permission to respond honestly to the requests and demands presented to us. We become confident enough to risk other people's displeasure if complying with their wishes is not in our own best interest.

May I say no today when that's what I mean.

Cherish the child within.

Whatever our chronological age, within each of us there is a spiritual child who can experience awe and wonder and mystery. The more we know, the more we realize how much we don't know. Led by our spiritual child, we can let our curiosity wander freely through the wide open spaces of our thoughts. We can set off on an expedition of exploration that will introduce us to the vast reaches of inner space.

Nurtured during periods of meditation, our spiritual child offers a sense of reverence to the deep moments of meaning that come upon us unexpectedly during the day. When allowed to develop, the spiritual child contributes an element of freshness to our tired, jaded sensibilities. We see the familiar scene with new vision.

A child is naturally humble and asks lots of questions. Our spiritual child asks questions about the meaning of life and our purpose in it. The pursuit of answers to these questions will unfold new dimensions of experience for us.

Today, I will nurture my spiritual child.

Shared secrets are no longer toxic.

Not all secrets are hazardous to our health. What I'm going to give you for your birthday can remain a secret for now without harming either of us. It's a temporary secret, and it's a nice one.

But if I try to keep my anger toward you a secret for fear of upsetting our relationship, that secret will begin to fester, poisoning the air between us. The secrets from my past of which I am ashamed interfere with my present serenity and fuel my eating disorder. They damage my self-esteem and drive wedges into my integrity.

I need to be known by another person. I need to be accepted in spite of those things I would prefer to hide. When I reveal my secrets to a trusted friend or counselor, I neutralize their toxic effect. A gradual process of healing takes place as more of me becomes available to both of us. When I share my secrets, I put myself back together.

If there are toxic secrets in my life today, I will begin the process of neutralizing them by sharing them.

*What we are goes further than what
we have.*

When we attempt to define ourselves by our possessions, we get caught up in the quest for more. The compulsion to amass more and more things, like the compulsion to eat more and more or to become thinner and thinner, is linked to our sense of inadequacy. When we don't respect ourselves as we are, then we feel we must acquire more in order to be acceptable.

If we don't like ourselves in a little house, we probably won't like ourselves in a big one either. Some of us who have lost many pounds, or who have gained to reach a healthy weight, are still unable to feel good about our bodies. The key lies not in the externals, the trappings, but in our internal sense of what kind of person we are.

Our values determine what we aspire to be. This is a matter between ourselves and a Higher Power, our definition of ultimate good. What we love, respect, and revere, we shall become. Wise choices lead to inner affirmation and peace.

Today, I will focus more clearly on what I am than on what I have.

Sometimes we need to learn something more than once.

Knowledge, even when it comes by way of painful experience, doesn't always stick. Some of us may find ourselves repeating an unhappy learning experience more than once before the message begins to affect our subsequent patterns of behavior. We remember, "Oh, yes, I tried that before, and it didn't work then either. I hope I won't have to try it again."

With luck, we won't. But if we do, we can treat ourselves with kindness. Another binge, another angry outburst, another mishandling of a relationship — we'd rather not repeat the pain, but here we are again, and gentle patience is the most constructive response.

Along with our commitment to recovery, we can make a commitment to accept ourselves wherever we are today. We're learning what works for us and what does not. When we're willing to repeat the lessons as many times as necessary until what works becomes automatic, we will eventually reach our goal.

I am willing to do today whatever it takes to get better.

Life flows — we don't need to push it.

Through practicing the Twelve Steps, we learn to trust life. We dare to believe that we will get what we need when we need it. That today's crises will shrink into relative insignificance next week. That we will make progress when we let ourselves be carried along by the forces of growth.

We become willing to believe that other people will do the best they can. That a Higher Power is taking care of them as well as us. That good will prevail.

We give up our white-knuckled efforts to control the flow of life. We stop trying to make it go faster when we're impatient and slower when we're enjoying ourselves.

When we can do these things, we find we're well on the way to recovery. Trusting that events will work out for the best in the long run means we do not have to overeat, purge, or starve in an attempt to make life go faster or better or in a different direction. We can relax and be enthusiastic participants in life as it unfolds each day, believing that our part will become clear to us one day at a time.

Instead of trying to push life today, I will let it carry me along, directed by a Higher Power.

If I'm smart, I won't try to fool myself.

Honesty is the bottom line of recovery. To get better, I must honestly face that I have a problem. I must be honest about my willingness to make the changes necessary in recovery, and honest about what I really think and feel.

Honesty costs. If I let myself know that the circumstances of a relationship violate my integrity, then I will need to act on that knowledge, and there will be a price to pay. If I admit I feel unfairly treated by a co-worker, I will need to decide how I will respond, which may involve confrontation. In both cases, it might appear to be less costly to fool myself into thinking all is fine, but the price of personal deception is loss of authenticity.

One thing I know: If I am not honest with myself, there will be a protest at some level of my awareness. A physical symptom, some emotional distress, or a general spiritual malaise will let me know I have not been fooled.

I will use the powerful tool of honesty today.

Are you afraid to succeed?

Something about success frightens many of us. Perhaps we fear the envy of others, that they will like us less. Maybe we don't want to prove our capabilities because if we do, we will be under pressure to continue living up to them. If we succeed, what more will be left to do, except perhaps to fail?

A poor self-image persuades us we don't deserve to succeed. The messages we have received from important others may have convinced us we'll never amount to anything, so why try? And if we don't succeed, we will have the payoff of feeling sorry for ourselves and not having to face the next challenge.

We need to determine if we are ready to risk success and are prepared for the changes that will accompany it.

The measure of true success is inner satisfaction. When considered in this light, success may mean ceasing to work for the approval of an audience and, instead, dedicating ourselves to the fulfillment of our heart's desires.

Today, I give myself permission to succeed.

When all else fails, turn it over.

Your job isn't working out, a family member is in trouble, you are depressed and don't know what to do. You talk to your boss, you encourage the family member to get counseling, you take a long walk and go over your options with a friend. When these remedies don't solve the problems, and when you've tried all the other possibilities you can think of and they don't work either, what do you do?

In Step Three we "made a decision to turn our will and our lives over to the care of God *as we understood Him.*" We don't merely take this Step once and then forget about it. We keep taking Step Three over and over again, especially when we encounter difficulties that have no readily apparent solution.

If something is troubling you today, you don't want to eat too much or too little, because you know neither will help. Why not give the program a chance to work for you? Why not use the support of a Higher Power? That support is always available — now. You can count on it.

Right now, I turn over what I cannot manage to my Higher Power.

*The drive to create propels us
forward.*

We do well to tend and celebrate our creative
instincts. They urge us toward self-expression,
whether we are painting a picture, listening to a
troubled friend, or programming a computer.
Each one of us is an original, and our mission is to
discover that originality, bring it to light, and
share it with others.

One of the major delights of recovery is the
continued unfolding of our creative power, in
whatever form it manifests itself. Some of us write
poems, some of us take pictures, some of us build
bridges, and some of us do all three. The myriad
ways in which we express our creativity run the
gamut from artistic endeavor, to mathematical
problem-solving, to entertaining a child on a
rainy day.

Channeling our creativity into the realm of human relationships is perhaps the most rewarding
route of all, and one that is open to each of us. We
can contribute our originality to the creation of a
friendship, a home, our family, our life.

*Today I will believe in my urge to create and al-
low it to find expression in the practical details of
my life.*

Feelings need to be expressed.

For many of us, feelings of anger, hurt, embarrassment, fear, and sadness are difficult to express. Consequently, we often turn to food in an attempt to make them go away.

I used to try to bury unpleasant feelings with food. That didn't work. Now, if I don't find a way of talking about whatever it is that has me worried or upset or disappointed, the bad feeling will swirl around in my consciousness. I will get stuck in thinking, "What if? Why didn't I? How could I have been so stupid? How could you have been so mean?"

If I talk about what's bothering me, I can reach a better understanding and acceptance of the problem, and I can get rid of my obsession with it. The anger, embarrassment, hurt, fear, or sadness passes. For me, sharing my feelings with someone else, along with turning them over to a Higher Power, is a necessary part of maintaining abstinence.

May I continue to learn how to express my feelings constructively.

There is a middle ground between being a marshmallow and being a porcupine.

Part of our problem might have been an over-developed set of antennae for picking up other people's feelings and reactions. If it was, we do not have to swing wildly to the other direction and erect a prickly defense that does not permit anyone to get close. We can learn to sort out our own legitimate needs and feelings from the signals and demands we receive from others. We can be accessible without permitting ourselves to be steamrolled.

We will find that the people close to us can appreciate and respect our boundaries when we assert them firmly and with inner conviction. Without attacking someone else and without being abrasively defensive, we can learn to state our opinions, preferences, and needs.

The art of interpersonal relations is a constant challenge. As we come to feel more secure in our own individuality, we refine and polish our skills.

I will steer a middle course today between being overly compliant and refusing to bend.

*Thank goodness I don't have to do
this alone!*

If left entirely to my own devices, I would probably still be waking up every morning saying,
"Today, I'm not going to binge; I will stick to my
diet." And it's also probable that I would still be
bingeing before noon.

A combination of embarrassment and pride
makes us feel we should solve our problems by
ourselves, without asking for help — alone
against the world. This kind of thinking cuts us off
from the resources that are available to us, and we
turn to food instead of people for help. As our illness progresses, the problems get worse instead
of better. Trying to manage our difficulties alone
is a little like walking through a strange house at
night with the lights off. We may be proud that we
were able to stay on our feet from the front door
to the back door, but how many collisions did we
have?

Now we know how to turn on the lights. We are
not alone in the dark. An OA meeting, a friend, a
doctor, a moment of inspiration from a Power
greater than ourselves — support is ours for the
asking, provided we ask.

I will reach out for the support I need today.

*A family is only as healthy as its
members.*

Our family system has an impact on us, just as
we have an impact on it. The family affects our
eating disorder, and our eating disorder affects
the family. Our dysfunctions are interrelated.

During the initial stages of recovery, we may be
more prone to consider how our family has affected us. As we move along, a positive sign is our
increasing ability to understand the impact our
eating behavior has had on our parents, siblings,
spouse, and children. We have not been easy to
live with, and the implications are far-reaching.
Our progress in recovery, though, may be a catalyst that starts family healing.

When we gain insight and move away from destructive habits, we encourage those around us to
grow too. Old patterns of garbled communication, blaming, and overdependency do not fit our
new goals. Our work to get better can motivate
those we love to also seek help and make changes.
Though a stronger, healthier family system may
be the outcome, I need to remember that I'm only
responsible for my effort in recovery.

*Today, I will be sensitive to my part in the dy-
namics of my family.*

Denying a fact does not make it go away.

Many of us deny what we don't want to face. We may wear layer upon layer of clothing to try to hide an emaciated body. We may block out certain aspects of our appearance when we look in a mirror. Or, we may refuse to face the fact of a serious illness, an impending move, or the end of a relationship.

From time to time, we all play ostrich, burying our heads and refusing to see what is right in front of us. Denial is part of addiction; also, it is often the first stage in our reaction to tragedy. For a brief period, denial may cushion the shock of trauma, but then we must let reality in if we are to operate in the real world and honestly deal with the problem.

The Steps begin healing us by piercing our denial. They continue by suggesting specific actions that keep us anchored in the reality of what we need to do to get well. Our program gives us the strength and support to confront the difficult facts of our everyday existence without denying them in the vain hope that they will disappear.

I am strong enough to face what is real today.

If we're hearing static from the past,
we can switch to a different frequency.

Have you heard an old authoritarian voice in your head that monopolizes your attention, tells you what to do, and criticizes the way you do it? Do you keep up a running argument with the voice? Comply with its orders? Or vacillate between rebellion and submission?

Sometimes the voices from our past are supportive, affirming our efforts and boosting our confidence. These are the ones we want to listen to often. The others, negative and self-deprecating voices we can do without. We can learn to screen out the static from the past that pops and crackles and distracts us from what's going on in the present. We can learn to switch our attention from the negative voices to the positive message of recovery.

We do not have to take orders from the past. We are responsible now for making our own decisions in harmony with the will of a Higher Power that gives guidance but does not coerce. Prayer and meditation tune us in to a frequency that is static-free.

Today, I will take care of myself by being responsive to the voices of the present.

*We can't eliminate stress, but we
can tame it.*

Stress goes along with being alive. Without it,
we would be like a bowl of Jell-O. Stress is good
for us when it motivates us to action, to deeds and
accomplishment, to the exertion of our best efforts. Stress is not good when it interferes with
our ability to function, when we feel blocked and
tight, up against the wall.

An overload of stress curdles our good times. If
we're not going to medicate tension with food or
restricting, what can we do? For one thing, we can
carefully check our priorities to determine if some
of the stress we're experiencing is unnecessary.

We may discover that we are trying to do too
many things and that a false sense of duty is impos-
ing needless obligations on us.

Having our priorities in order goes a long way
toward taming stress. So do getting enough rest
and exercise and eating the right amounts of the
right kinds of food. Beyond that, we can accept
the reality that we will have stressful times, and
know that we also have a constant source of peace
and support to carry us through.

---

*To tame today's stress, I will breathe deeply
through my spiritual center.*

Abstinence is a gift that keeps on giving.

We cherish life by eating for health. By taking care of ourselves, we become able to care for others.

Many of us have memories of holiday indulgences that brought a net loss to ourselves and those dear to us. Although excess seemed exciting and moderation dull, we have found that overindulgence produces dullness of body and spirit. And we have discovered that moderation is the gateway to abundant life.

We believe this gift of abstinence comes from a Power greater than ourselves. It often comes quietly without fanfare, when we prepare ourselves to receive it. It comes as an outgrowth of love, for ourselves and for others.

Today's abstinence is a gift we can share with others who are recovering. We can use it to make ourselves accessible to the needs and feelings of our family and friends. We can use it to make our work more fulfilling and our recreation more fun. We can use it to grow spiritually.

With abstinence, the gifts of the season are mine to share.

Celebrate the process of recovering.

We may not be there yet, but we're on our way. We can celebrate today's new step in our journey toward recovery. We can celebrate with love. We can celebrate with abstinence.

If today is not as merry or as joyful as we would like, perhaps we should take a look at our expectations. Perhaps we cling to unrealistic visions of gleaming perfection that make the more subdued glow of actuality pale by comparison. The way out of that trap may be to accept serenity as our goal rather than ecstasy.

Undergirding our celebration of special days is the ongoing process of getting better through a spiritual program. When the holiday glitter is gone, the program will still be here for us, structuring our progress.

So we can make merry, knowing we are celebrating in depth, celebrating the good things we have now and the good that comes into our lives each day as we follow the Steps toward recovery.

Today and every day is cause for celebration and an opportunity to make progress.

Health, not illness, is the design of creation.

Sometimes we become so accustomed to maladaptive behavior that we begin to think it's normal. Our eating disorder developed as a way of coping that may have been the best response we could have made to the problems we faced at the time. In spite of the inconvenience, we got used to the disorder. But we all know now that the extremes of starving and bingeing are neither normal nor desirable. And we are coming to believe that the creative power of health is on our side.

If we have learned unsatisfactory responses, we can unlearn them. We have more resources now than we did when we were younger. Even though we can't control other people or situations, we can choose ways of getting our needs met that do not damage our bodies or our self-esteem. We can act in cooperation with the forces of health.

We do this each time we follow a reasonable food plan. We move toward health and away from disorder when we make decisions based on spiritual insights and allow the natural order of creation to manifest itself in our lives.

Today, I will let health and order direct my behavior.

More is not necessarily the answer.

We often think that if a little is good, more will be better, or that if we are not happy, it must be because we don't have enough of something.

Wanting and craving. The desire for what we don't have prevents us from appreciating and enjoying what we do have — right now, this moment. We often sell ourselves continual dissatisfaction by focusing on what we appear to lack. When we do, we let food become a symbol for all the things we think we want but don't possess.

Our heads know that eating more than our bodies need for nourishment and energy makes us fat and unhappy. Our heads also know that compulsive dieting to a weight less than normal is not the answer either.

So how much is enough? Can we learn to savor the blessings we have now, today? Do we really need more, or do we need to fully experience the gifts of the present?

I can always want more, but today I will concentrate on what I have right now.

We can trust the seasons of life.

It is a Power greater than ourselves that cycles our experience. By listening closely to the internal promptings that direct our growth, we cooperate with this Power. We go through seasons of great effort, seasons of turbulence, seasons of peace, seasons of despair, seasons of apathy, seasons of decisiveness. Short or long, the individual season runs its course, bears its fruit, and evolves into the next phase of our development.

Just as we learn to trust the stability of the natural world and believe that spring will follow winter, so, too, do we come to believe that there is a dependable rhythm to our growth. If we go through a period when our emotions seem ice-bound, we trust a thaw will come. A time of indecision may be a necessary transition to a new phase of activity.

Reluctance to pass through an appointed season frustrates our development. There is nothing to fear except our own fear of becoming who we are meant to be. Our inner almanac contains the knowledge we need in order to plant and harvest each season's crop.

I will say yes today to the power that cycles my experience.

Out of disorder, a plan for living.

Our journey toward recovery began at the point where we recognized how unmanageable life had become. Food seemed to be the problem — either we ate too much or we ate too little — and the obsession with weight and diet threatened to take over the rest of our existence.

So we sought help. We embraced a simple program that addresses not only the problem of what and how much to eat but also the unmanageability of life in general when we are not operating from our spiritual center. The Twelve Steps lead us to a new understanding of how the spiritual component can introduce order and reliability into all aspects of our everyday routine.

We adopt the principles of Twelve Step living at our own individual pace, as we see their relevance and become ready to accept them. The healing power of spiritual awareness permeates our consciousness little by little, and we find that the wisdom of the program can structure our relationships and our work as well as our attitude toward food.

I will allow my spiritual awareness to structure my plan for living today.

You think you've got troubles?

No matter how bad things are, they probably could be worse. Our malfunctioning furnace or air conditioner seems less of a catastrophe when we hear about thousands of people left homeless because of an earthquake or flood. And the survivors are lucky to be alive.

Intellectually, we know this, but at another level we may still feel sorry for ourselves, sorry because our job is dull, or we're alone, or money is tight, or we're too fat, or we're misunderstood — we can always find a reason for self-pity.

Spending time and energy feeling sorry for ourselves distracts us from the goal of recovery. A detour into self-pity is a no-win strategy, one we can reject immediately, before it begins to stalemate our forward momentum.

Today's troubles can lead to tomorrow's victories if we use them as a springboard to courage, self-discipline, and inner strength.

Instead of feeling sorry for myself today, I will use my troubles as building blocks of recovery.

Time is a circle. The end is the beginning.

Day by day, a year comes and goes. Today's end is the beginning of the rest of our lives. We take with us what we have learned today. We are the same and not the same.

As long as we are alive, we will continue to wrestle with questions, seek answers, solve problems. Let's be gentle with ourselves and others, choosing to respond with nonjudging love and acceptance instead of unrealistic demands of perfection.

We have found a blueprint for recovery. Our preoccupation with not enough and too much has led us to a spiritual solution. Each day brings us new opportunities to express our development — a more patient response to a traffic jam, the ability to empathize with a child's embarrassment, the acceptance of a disappointment. Today is another day to learn how to be serene, to nurture body and spirit so that we may function as an integrated totality. We will continue to learn and grow toward recovery.

I will begin and end today by listening to my inner voice.

INDEX

NOTES

NOTES

NOTES

NOTES

NOTES

NOTES

Hazelden Publishing offers an array of daily meditation books, in print and e-book formats, to be read in the morning, at night, or anytime. Whether one is a recovering addict, sponsor, or counselor, there is a meditation book suitable for all. Our books cover recovery topics pertinent to everyone (*Twenty-Four Hours a Day, Keep It Simple, The Promise of a New Day*), as well as daily meditations written especially for men (*Touchstones*), women (*Each Day a New Beginning*), teens (*Twenty-Four Hours for Teens*), adult children (*Days of Healing, Days of Joy*), families (*Today's Gift*), those dealing with codependency (*The Language of Letting Go*), mental health issues (*A Restful Mind*), eating disorders (*Inner Harvest*), sex addiction (*Answers in the Heart*), and more.

Hazelden Publishing meditation books are available at fine bookstores everywhere. To order from Hazelden Publishing, call **800-328-9000** or visit **hazelden.org/bookstore**.